Shaped by FAITH

40-DAY DEVOTIONAL

Strengthening Your Spirit, Mind, & Body

THERESA ROWE

Copyright ©2025 Theresa Rowe, Shaped By Faith

All rights reserved. No part of this publication may be reproduced, stored in a retrieval system or transmitted in any form or by any means, electronic, mechanical, including photocopying, recording, or otherwise without prior written consent from the publisher.

Formatted and edited by Katie Erickson, KatieEricksonEditing.com

Unless otherwise indicated, all Scripture quotations are taken from the *Holy Bible*, New Living Translation, copyright © 1996, 2004, 2015 by Tyndale House Foundation. Used by permission of Tyndale House Publishers, Inc., Carol Stream, Illinois 60188. All rights reserved.

Scriptures marked NIV taken from THE HOLY BIBLE, NEW INTERNATIONAL VERSION®, NIV® Copyright © 1973, 1978, 1984, 2011 by Biblica, Inc.® Used by permission. All rights reserved worldwide.

Scriptures marked NKJV taken from the New King James Version®. Copyright © 1982 by Thomas Nelson. Used by permission. All rights reserved.

ISBN 979-8-9930089-0-5

Dedication

To **Jehovah Rapha**, the Lord who heals – thank You for restoring my spirit, mind, and body for Your purposes. Every breath, step, and word in this devotional is for Your glory.

To my husband, Robin – my anchor in love and faith, my steadfast encourager, and my greatest earthly blessing. Thank you for believing in me and standing by my side in every season.

To my children and grandchildren – you are treasured gifts from God, bringing joy to my days and constant reminders of His faithfulness.

To my Shaped By Faith students, my media team, my online community, and my prayer warriors – your encouragement strengthens my heart for this mission.

To my editor, Katie Erickson – thank you for refining these words so they can inspire others for His glory.

And to every reader – may you know His strength, His healing, and His greater purpose for your life.

Using scripture, life experience, prayer, and simple exercise, Theresa Rowe's *Shaped By Faith* devotional book offers everything needed to step into a new life with Christ as she leads readers step-by-faithful-step to strengthen their physical, mental, and spiritual health.

Tracy Crump
Editor, codirector of Write Life Workshops, and author of Health, Healing, and Wholeness: Devotions of Hope in the Midst of Illness

Shaped By Faith 40-Day Devotional: Strengthening Your Spirit, Mind, & Body is so much more than just a devotional. It is a detailed plan to grow your faith, enrich your mind, and strengthen your body. Theresa Rowe's testimony of health and heart struggles will inspire your own path towards physical and spiritual transformation.

Sharon Wilharm
Author of Women of Prayer *Bible study and host of "All God's Women" podcast and syndicated radio show*

I absolutely recommend this inspirational devotional. It's an easy-to-follow format that covers you in prayer, power, and peace. I love the daily prayers and personal testimonies. Every day is now a journey of overcoming with Jesus, strengthening my body, and shaping my faith. Theresa has such an honest and authentic approach. I enjoy that each day is greeted with hope and encouragement. This is a kingdom-led journey that changes more than your body but also your relationship with God.

Angela Hollon
Co-Founder of Set Apart Farms and Creator of Herbs of the Torah

It's a true blessing to endorse *Shaped By Faith 40-Day Devotional: Strengthening Your Spirit, Mind, & Body* by my dear friend, Theresa Rowe. Theresa's devotional stands apart, as she invites you to see physical fitness through a fresh, faith-filled lens. As you embark on this 40-day journey, you will sense Theresa walking beside you, encouraging you daily in both the physical and the spiritual.

By blending scripture with movement, you'll begin to experience how the Word of God is truly living and active–working on your behalf to bring transformation and healing from the inside out. Receive a fresh revelation of Jesus' great love for you through this powerful devotional–reviving your spirit, energizing your body, and bringing rest to your soul.

Christine Vales
Christine Vales Ministries,
Author of *His Appointed Times*

I was first introduced to Theresa Rowe through her *Shaped By Faith* television broadcast. Her beautiful spirit, miraculous journey, and deep desire to inspire God's people to fulfill His purpose have touched and encouraged our viewers for nearly a decade.

Her newest project, *Shaped By Faith 40-Day Devotional: Strengthening Your Spirit, Mind, & Body*, is sure to draw readers into a Christ-centered lifestyle–spirit, mind, and body–leading to a more fulfilling walk with the Lord.

Debra Fraser
President of TLN Media

In *Shaped By Faith 40-Day Devotional: Strengthening Your Spirit, Mind, & Body*, Theresa Rowe brings the same unique and powerful voice that has inspired viewers on Global7.tv. She skillfully combines faith, fitness, and everyday encouragement to uplift both body and soul.

Her message is biblically grounded, full of grace, and speaks directly to the challenges believers face in today's world. Through personal stories, Scripture, and practical exercises, Theresa equips readers to honor God not only with their spiritual walk but also with their physical health and daily habits. I am honored to recommend this devotional and thank God for the impact He continues to make through Theresa's ministry.

Enkelejda Shelburne
CEO, Global7.tv

Theresa Rowe is the real deal—her life radiates the very message she shares in *Shaped By Faith*. This devotional is not just words on a page; it's a life-tested roadmap to strengthening your spirit, mind, and body through God's truth. She has woven together two worlds often kept apart—faith and fitness. Her journey is a testimony to God's power to redeem, heal, renew, transform, and make all things new.

I've seen firsthand the fruit of her life and the joy she carries, and I can tell you – this collection of daily scriptures and stories will inspire, equip, lead, and encourage you from the inside out.

Jennifer Mallan
Author and TV host of "Come Home with Jen Mallan"

In her devotional book, *Shaped By Faith: A 40-Day Devotional for Strengthening Your Spirit, Mind, & Body*, Theresa Rowe offers guidance for spiritual growth, but she doesn't stop there. She goes on to suggest ways to get into physical shape as well. Her personal stories were inspiring, the shared Scriptures meaningful, and the suggested exercises practical. In helpful, easy-to-understand steps, Theresa shares how to improve your balance and strengthen your physical body while stressing the power of our faith in the Lord to improve us in every way. Each day's devotional will motivate you to get stronger in mind, body, and faith.

Ann H. Gabhart
Author of *The Pursuit of Elena Bradford*

Table of Contents

Introduction: Shaped By Faith, My Journey 1

Week 1: Strength for the Journey 5
    Day 1: Strength for the Journey 7
    Day 2: Faith Over Fear 13
    Day 3: Breaking Chains – Overcoming Obstacles 19
    Day 4: Strength Through Surrender 25
    Day 5: Disciplined for God's Purpose 31
    Day 6: Victory in Christ 35
    Day 7: Faith in Action 39

Week 2: Realignment and Renewal 43
    Day 8: Pressing On 45
    Day 9: Getting Into Alignment 49
    Day 10: A Well-Watered Garden 53
    Day 11: Identity & Preventing Identity Theft 57
    Day 12: Guard Your Heart 61
    Day 13: Honoring God with the Body 65
    Day 14: Where Faith Meets Fitness 71

Week 3: Drawing Closer to God 75
    Day 15: Drawing Closer to God 77
    Day 16: My Morning Wake-Up Call 81
    Day 17: Devouring the Word 85
    Day 18: Keeping Your Head Over Your Heart 89
    Day 19: The Heart of a Healthy Marriage 93
    Day 20: The Face of Grace 97
    Day 21: Can You Hear Me Now? 101

Week 4: Walking It Out at Home 105
    Day 22: The Great Commission Starts at Home 107
    Day 23: Move Forward by Faith 111
    Day 24: Tick-Tock, Tock-Tick 117
    Day 25: Pressing On with Endurance 121
    Day 26: God Makes All Things New 125

Day 27: Living Victoriously in Christ 129
Day 28: Finishing Strong 135

Week 5: Staying the Course 139
Day 29: Honoring God with Every Rep 141
Day 30: The Heart of God 147
Day 31: The Joy of the Lord is My Strength 151
Day 32: Living for Jesus – The Next Generation 155
Day 33: There is Purpose in Our Pain 161
Day 34: Do Not Quit 165
Day 35: Matters of the Heart – Aligning Our Emotions with God's Will 171

Week 6: Finishing Strong...177
Day 36: God's Recipe Includes Lots of Love – Strengthening Family Bonds 179
Day 37: Faith-Prayer-Discipline-Repeat 185
Day 38: Rooted in Spiritual Habits..191
Day 39: Persevering in Purpose... 195
Day 40: Finish Strong with a Kingdom Mindset 199

Conclusion: Keep Moving Forward in the Strength of the Lord.... 205

Encouragement to Keep Going... 207

A Final Blessing 209

Next Steps: Living Shaped By Faith...211

My Reflections & Prayer Notes 213

Stay Connected with Shaped By Faith 215

From My Heart to Yours 217

About the Author 220

Introduction: Shaped By Faith, My Journey

A Childhood Church of Thorns

As a child, I had no idea that God was already preparing me for a future in ministry and faith-based fitness. In the most unlikely place–deep within the thick sticker bushes behind our home–I started what would later become known in my heart as THE STICKER BUSH CHURCH. I gathered the neighborhood children, preached to them with childlike passion, and then led them through a physical challenge, something active and fun to go along with the message. At the time, it felt like simple play, but looking back, I realized it was something sacred. God was planting seeds of boldness, creativity, and purpose. He was shaping my faith even then, showing me that He can use anything, even a patch of thorns, to prepare us for His calling. What began as a backyard adventure was really the beginning of SHAPED BY FAITH.

A Heart Strengthened by Faith

Faith and fitness became deeply personal when I faced my own battles. I was born with three holes in my heart, a congenital defect that required two open-heart surgeries: the first in November 1987, the second in September 2007. That journey was about more than physical survival; it became a path of spiritual transformation. God didn't just sustain me—He strengthened me, refined my faith, and shaped me for the calling He placed on my life.

I thank God every day for saving me twice: once through surgery, and ultimately through His grace.

I also experienced a miraculous healing from endometriosis, a condition that once caused intense suffering. Through prayer, faith, and God's mercy, I was completely healed. That healing deepened my trust in His power to restore, renew, and transform every part of our lives—spirit, mind, and body.

Shaped By Faith

These experiences taught me that true fitness is not just about the body—it's about aligning our spirit, mind, and body with God's Word. This 40-day devotional is designed to help you strengthen your faith as you strengthen your body. Each day, you'll find:

- **Scripture Focus** – A Bible verse to meditate on and apply.
- **Faith in Motion** – A personal story to inspire and encourage you.

- **Shaping Bodies & Hearts** – A faith and fitness parallel connecting spiritual truths with your wellness journey.
- **Shaping Bodies** – A simple physical exercise to support your health.
- **Shaping Hearts** – A spiritual exercise to deepen your walk with God.
- **Dig Deeper** – A daily challenge to put your faith and fitness into action.
- **Reflection & Prayer** – A moment to connect with the Lord.

This 40-day journey reflects the biblical pattern of transformation, preparation, and renewal—offering time and space for God to shape your spirit, mind, and body from the inside out.

Just as a potter molds clay, God is continually shaping us. He is forming us into His image, refining our character, and strengthening us for His purposes. This devotional is an invitation to let Him shape you—inside and out. Get ready to move, grow, and be transformed!

Week 1: Strength for the Journey

Scripture Focus:
"Commit everything you do to the Lord. Trust Him, and He will help you." (Psalm 37:5)

Weekly Focus:
This week, lay your foundation. Let the Lord strengthen you as you begin the journey—spirit, mind, and body. He walks beside you every step.

Weekly Prayer:
Lord, I give You these next seven days. Help me grow in strength, truth, and trust. Shape my heart to follow You fully. Amen.

Day 1: Strength for the Journey

Scripture Focus: "The Lord is my strength and my shield; my heart trusts in Him, and He helps me. My heart leaps for joy, and with my song I praise Him." (Psalm 28:7 NIV)

Faith in Motion: God's Grace Brings Strength

Years ago, I faced a life-altering moment—a gut punch that nearly knocked me down. My ex-husband, who often disappeared for entire weekends, walked into our home one morning and casually announced, "Don't take it personally, but I don't want to be married to you anymore." The pain and shock were real, but in that moment, I did the only thing I knew to do: I cried out to God.

I heard one word: **Go.**

So, I did. I picked up my six-month-old twins, walked out the door, and left my home completely unaware of how I would make it. But God knew. He placed people in my path, like Pearl, a childcare worker at the YMCA where I taught fitness classes. Her love and support were part of God's grace in my life. I stepped into my fitness class that day, feeling broken but determined, and led my students with the most faith-filled energy I had ever given. I didn't share my burden with them—I gave it to God, and in return, He gave me peace and strength to move forward.

For five years, I raised my children as a single mother, relying solely on God's provision. Every need was met, every prayer answered in His perfect time. I learned firsthand that when we surrender our struggles to Him, He sustains us, providing both grace and peace.

Shaping Bodies & Hearts: Our Strength Comes From God

Have you ever started a fitness journey with great enthusiasm, only to feel discouraged when progress seems slow? Maybe you've been eager to grow in your faith but struggle to stay consistent. Whether it's physical training or spiritual discipline, our strength comes from the Lord, not just our efforts.

Just as we train our bodies to build endurance and flexibility, we must also train our hearts and minds to trust in God's provision. Our faith is like a muscle—it requires regular exercise, nourishment, and time to grow. When we rely on God as our source of strength, we don't have to push through on our own. He sustains us when we feel weak, renews our spirits when we're weary, and equips us for every challenge ahead.

Shaping Bodies: Walking in Strength and Prayer

Walking is a gentle yet powerful way to begin building strength—physically and spiritually. It engages your legs, improves circulation, supports joint health, and lifts your mood. Best of all, it gives you space to connect with God as you move forward—literally and spiritually.

Exercise: 10-15 Minute Prayer Walk

- Find a peaceful path (outdoors or indoors).
- Walk with good posture: head tall, shoulders back, and core gently engaged ("navel to spine").
- As you walk, breathe deeply and speak to God. Praise Him. Thank Him. Ask for strength and direction.
- Use each step as a declaration: *"The Lord is my strength and my shield."*
- Let your walk become an act of worship and surrender.

This is your starting point. You're not just walking, you're stepping into strength, one faithful step at a time.

Shaping Hearts: Strengthening Your Faith

Trust in His Strength – When you feel weak or overwhelmed, remind yourself that God is your shield. Instead of striving in your power, surrender your struggles to Him.

Stay Consistent – Just as daily exercise builds physical strength, daily time in God's Word builds spiritual endurance. Start with a short passage and meditate on its truth.

Encourage Others – Strength isn't just for yourself; it's meant to be shared. Find a friend who may be struggling and speak words of encouragement over them. Together, you'll grow stronger in faith and fitness.

Dig Deeper

This is your starting point—where faith meets action. Each day, use this section to apply what you've read and let God shape your spirit, mind, and body. Journal how God is strengthening you as you meditate on Psalm 28:7, "The Lord is my strength and my shield."

Reflection & Prayer

Heavenly Father, thank You for being my strength and my shield. Help me to trust You fully, knowing that You will sustain me through every challenge I face. Strengthen my body as I train physically and renew my spirit as I grow in faith. Let my heart leap for joy as I praise You in all I do. In Jesus' name, amen.

My Reflections & Prayer Notes:

My Reflections & Prayer Notes

Day 2: Faith Over Fear

Scripture Focus: "For God has not given us a spirit of fear and timidity, but of power, love, and self-discipline." (2 Timothy 1:7 NKJV)

Faith in Motion: Overcoming Fear Through Faith

Fear has a way of creeping into our lives—sometimes in the form of small anxieties, other times as overwhelming burdens that paralyze us. But God calls us to walk in faith, not fear. When we place our trust in Him, fear loses its power over us. His Word reassures us that He has given us strength, love, and a sound mind to combat fear's grip.

One afternoon, my young grandson was playing in my home, a place filled with light from every window. Yet, despite the brightness, he was gripped with fear—afraid of shadows, afraid to be alone. If I sat in the same room, he played contentedly, but the moment I left, panic would take hold.

As I returned to comfort him, I was reminded of my childhood fears—how the enemy used fear as a weapon to keep me from peace. But I also remembered the moment I invited Jesus to take up residence in my heart. That was when fear lost its power over me. It was time for my grandson to understand that he had nothing to fear, for God was with him.

I knelt beside him and told him the truth: God is always near. I reminded him of Matthew 18:10, which speaks of the angels assigned to watch over children, and of 2 Timothy 1:7, which promises that fear does not come from God. He listened intently, and his heart began to settle.

Fear is a powerful emotion, but it does not have to rule our lives. Whether we are children afraid of the dark or adults facing uncertain futures, we must lean into God's truth. He calls us to trust in Him, and in that trust, we find peace.

Shaping Bodies & Hearts: Finding Balance in Fear

When fear takes hold, it throws us off balance—spiritually and even physically. Just like fear makes our faith unsteady, a lack of balance in our bodies can make us weak and prone to falling. Strengthening our physical balance helps us stand firm, just as strengthening our faith helps us remain steady in life's storms.

When you practice balance exercises, you must engage your core, focus your mind, and stand firm. Likewise, when fear tries to shake you, you must engage your faith, focus on God's truth, and stand firm on His promises. The more you train your body to balance, the stronger and steadier you become—just like your faith grows stronger as you trust in God instead of fear.

Shaping Bodies: Steadying the Body & Mind

Balance and stability exercises help us stay steady, just as faith keeps us grounded when fear tries to shake us. This simple exercise will remind you to stand firm in faith even when fear attempts to throw you off balance.

Exercise: Single-Leg Balance Hold

- Stand tall with hip-width feet apart.
- Slowly lift one foot off the ground and balance on the opposite leg.
- Hold for 30 seconds, then switch legs.
- To increase difficulty, close your eyes and focus on steady breathing.
- As you hold your balance, meditate on **2 Timothy 1:7**.

Just as your body learns to stabilize, let God's truth steady your heart and mind against fear.

Shaping Hearts: Strengthening Faith Over Fear

Declare God's Promises – Speak His truth over your fear. Say aloud, "I do not have a spirit of fear, but of power, love, and a sound mind." (2 Timothy 1:7)

Pray Through Fear – Instead of letting fear take control, pray about what is troubling you and surrender it to God.

Step Forward in Faith – Do one thing today that challenges your fear. Whether it's speaking boldly, trusting God with a decision, or encouraging someone else, take a step of faith.

Dig Deeper

Practice the balance exercise and spend time meditating on **2 Timothy 1:7**. Write down one fear you are surrendering to God this week, and journal how He is giving you peace in return.

Reflection & Prayer

Heavenly Father, I know that fear does not come from You. Help me to lean into Your strength when I feel anxious. Remind me that You are always near and that I am never alone. Strengthen my heart and mind so that I may walk boldly in faith, trusting You every step of the way. Amen.

My Reflections & Prayer Notes:

Day 3: Breaking Chains – Overcoming Obstacles

Scripture Focus: "So if the Son sets you free, you will be free indeed." (John 8:36 NIV)

Faith in Motion: Breaking Free from the Past

Obstacles come in many forms—fear, self-doubt, past failures, and even physical limitations. These chains can hold us back, making us feel stuck, but Jesus came to set us free. When we surrender our struggles to Him, He provides the strength we need to break through the barriers in our lives.

There was a time in my life when I carried a heavy burden of unforgiveness and self-doubt. I felt as though I was running a race with weights tied to my ankles, unable to move forward. I had been deeply hurt by people I trusted, and instead of releasing those hurts to God, I held onto them tightly. The weight of bitterness grew heavier each day.

One day, during a workout, I realized how much my spiritual weight mirrored my physical endurance. Just as extra weight slows movement and causes exhaustion, so does unforgiveness weigh down the spirit. God opened my eyes to see that I was the one holding the chains. I had the key to freedom in my hands all along: forgiveness and surrender. The moment I truly gave those burdens to Christ, I felt lighter, stronger, and free.

God calls us to release the things that hold us back so that we can run the race He has set before us. When we trust Him to remove the roadblocks, we will find new strength to overcome any obstacle.

Shaping Bodies & Hearts: Strength Comes Through Resistance

In fitness, resistance training is essential for building strength. Lifting weights challenges muscles to grow stronger, just as overcoming obstacles strengthens our faith. The struggles we face are like weights—we can either let them hold us down or use them to build endurance and resilience.

Just as resistance training helps our muscles adapt and grow, the challenges we face in life are opportunities to strengthen our faith. When we push through difficulties with God's strength, we develop spiritual endurance and perseverance. Instead of viewing obstacles as setbacks, we can see them as training grounds where our faith is fortified.

Shaping Bodies: Moving Forward in Faith

This movement builds strength in your back and shoulders—just as releasing our burdens to God strengthens our spirit and allows us to move forward in faith.

Exercise: Resistance Band Rows

- Stand with your feet hip-width apart and place the center of a resistance band securely under both feet.
- Hold one end of the band in each hand, arms extended in front of you.
- Bend your knees slightly and hinge forward at your hips, keeping your spine long and core engaged.
- Pull the band back in a rowing motion, keeping your elbows close to your body.
- Squeeze your shoulder blades together at the top, then slowly return to the starting position.
- Perform 3 sets of 12 controlled repetitions.

As you pull the band back, imagine pulling away from the chains of your past and stepping into the freedom God has for you.

Shaping Hearts: Releasing Burdens to God

Identify What's Holding You Back – What emotional or spiritual chains do you need to break?

Pray for Release – Ask God to help you let go of past hurts, fears, or self-doubt.

Speak God's Truth – Declare **John 8:36** over your life: "If the Son sets you free, you will be free indeed."

Move Forward – Take one physical and spiritual step today toward overcoming your obstacle—whether it's reaching out in forgiveness, starting a new fitness habit, or trusting God with a fear.

Dig Deeper

Practice the resistance band row throughout the week. As you move, reflect on one area where you need a breakthrough. Surrender it to God, and if you'd like, write down how He's strengthening your body and spirit as you walk in freedom.

Reflection & Prayer

Heavenly Father, I surrender every burden that has held me back. I no longer want to be weighed down by fear, unforgiveness, or self-doubt. Thank You for setting me free through Jesus. Strengthen my body and spirit as I move forward in faith, trusting You to break every chain in my life. Amen.

My Reflections & Prayer Notes:

My Reflections & Prayer Notes

Day 4: Strength Through Surrender

Scripture Focus: "For all who are led by the Spirit of God are children of God. So you have not received a spirit that makes you fearful slaves. Instead, you received God's Spirit when he adopted you as his own children. Now we call him, 'Abba, Father.'" (Romans 8:14-15)

Faith in Motion: Adopted by God

We often think of strength as pushing harder, doing more, and taking control, but true strength comes through surrendering to God. When we let go of our fears, our need for control, and our past wounds, we open ourselves to receive the full measure of God's power.

I was adopted when I was six weeks old and again at the age of twenty-six. My second adoption took place when I fully surrendered my life to Christ and embraced Him as my heavenly Father. My spiritual adoption was far greater than anything I could have imagined. I had spent much of my life yearning for love, putting up walls, and fearing rejection. I feared that if I gave my heart fully to anyone—

including my adoptive parents—I might be abandoned again.

As I carried this fear into adulthood, it affected my relationships, my decisions, and even my faith. But at God's perfect timing, He placed people in my life who showed me compassion and love, reminding me that I no longer had to live in fear. When I finally let go and surrendered to Christ, the shield of abandonment fell away, and I truly understood what it meant to be a child of God.

My story is a testimony that God adopts each of us into His family when we surrender ourselves to Him. We no longer have to live as spiritual orphans; we have a Father who will never leave us nor forsake us. When we understand our true identity in Christ, we can stand strong, knowing we are fully loved, fully accepted, and never alone.

Shaping Bodies & Hearts: Letting Go to Gain Strength

In fitness, we often think more effort equals more strength, but sometimes, relaxation and flexibility are just as important. Muscles need time to recover to grow stronger, and our bodies need balance between effort and rest. Spiritually, letting go of control and trusting God is what allows us to gain true strength.

Shaping Bodies: The Discipline of Surrender

This classic core-strengthening exercise emphasizes breath control, endurance, and mental focus—mirroring how spiritual surrender requires discipline and trust in God's strength.

Exercise: The Pilates Hundred:

- Lie flat on your back with knees bent and feet flat, or extend your legs to a 45-degree angle for more challenge.
- Lift your head, neck, and shoulders off the mat, reaching your arms long by your sides, hovering just above the floor.
- Engage your core and begin pumping your arms up and down in a controlled rhythm.
- Inhale through your nose for 5 arm pumps, then exhale through your mouth for 5 arm pumps.
- Repeat this breathing cycle 10 times (totaling 100 pumps).
- Keep your gaze toward your knees and maintain steady breathing throughout.

As you breathe and move with intention, reflect on Romans 8:14-15. Just as your breath anchors your body, allow the Spirit of God to center your soul, reminding you that you are His—fully loved, fully led, and free.

Shaping Hearts: Releasing Control

Identify What You Need to Surrender – Is it fear, the past, self-doubt, or control?

Speak Truth Over Yourself – Remind yourself of **Romans 8:14-15**—You are God's child, fully loved and accepted.

Let Go Through Prayer – Physically open your hands as a symbol of releasing your burdens to God.

Embrace God's Presence – Take a moment of stillness, inviting God's peace into your heart.

Dig Deeper

Set aside time each day this week to return to the deep stretch and breath work. As you stretch, surrender a specific worry or burden to God. Record in your journal how your body and spirit respond as you trust Him more deeply.

Reflection & Prayer

Heavenly Father, I surrender my fears, my past, and my need for control. Thank You for adopting me into Your family and reminding me that I am fully loved. Help me to release every burden into Your hands and walk in the freedom of being Your child. Amen.

My Reflections & Prayer Notes:

Day 5: Disciplined for God's Purpose

Scripture Focus: "No discipline seems pleasant at the time, but painful. Later on, however, it produces a harvest of righteousness and peace for those who have been trained by it." (Hebrews 12:11 NIV)

Faith in Motion: The Discipline of Daniel

Discipline is the key to lasting transformation—both spiritually and physically. We may not always enjoy the process, but the rewards are undeniable. When we submit to God's discipline, He strengthens us, molds us, and prepares us for His greater purpose.

Daniel's story is a powerful example of self-discipline and devotion to God. Despite living in a foreign land with immense pressure to conform, Daniel remained steadfast. He chose to honor God even in his diet, refusing to eat the rich foods of the king's table and instead sustaining himself on what he knew would keep him physically and spiritually pure.

There was a time in my own life when I had to make a similar choice. I realized that in order to serve God fully, I needed to discipline my body and mind. That meant making consistent decisions that honored Him—whether in my eating habits, my fitness routine, or my daily spiritual walk. Just like Daniel, I had to stand firm even when it was hard, trusting that God's way would yield the best results.

Discipline isn't about restricting ourselves for the sake of rules; it's about aligning our lives with God's best. The more we exercise discipline in one area, the more it carries over into other parts of life.

Shaping Bodies & Hearts: The Power of Consistency

In fitness, results come from consistent effort over time. You don't see change after one workout; it's the daily discipline of showing up, even when you don't feel like it, that leads to transformation. The same is true in faith. Consistently spending time with God, obeying His Word, and trusting His process leads to a spiritually strong life.

Shaping Bodies: Core Strength Challenge

Your core is the foundation for balance, posture, and endurance. Just as physical strength begins at the core, spiritual strength is built through daily discipline and surrender to God.

Exercise: Plank Hold

- Begin in a push-up position with your body in a straight line from head to heels.
- Engage your core, draw your navel toward your spine, and hold steady.
- Breathe deeply and maintain good alignment.
- Hold the plank for **30 seconds to 1 minute**, depending on your ability.

As you hold, **meditate on Hebrews 12:11**, and let the challenge remind you that God's discipline is shaping you for lasting peace and strength.

Shaping Hearts: Strengthening Your Daily Discipline

Create a Spiritual Routine – Set aside consistent time for prayer and Bible study.

Be Accountable – Find a partner to encourage you in both faith and fitness.

Commit to Small Steps – Start with one small discipline today—whether waking up earlier to pray, drinking more water, or moving your body daily.

Dig Deeper

Choose one spiritual and one physical discipline to commit to daily this week. Write down your progress and reflect on how God is growing you through consistency.

Reflection & Prayer

Heavenly Father, I know that discipline isn't always easy, but I trust that Your ways are higher than mine. Help me to stay consistent in both my spiritual and physical life. Train me to be disciplined so that I may bear a harvest of righteousness and peace. Amen.

My Reflections & Prayer Notes:

Day 6: Victory in Christ

Scripture Focus: "No, in all these things we are more than conquerors through Him who loved us." (Romans 8:37 NIV)

Faith in Motion: Spiritual Anorexia

We all face battles of many kinds, but victory is ours in Christ because God has already won the war. Victory is about knowing that God has already won the war. When we walk in faith, we don't fight for victory; we fight from victory. Christ has overcome, and through Him, we are more than conquerors.

There was a time in my life when I was spiritually starving. I was trying to sustain myself on surface-level faith—attending church, saying quick prayers, and hoping that was enough. But inside, I was malnourished. I wasn't feeding on God's Word. I wasn't equipping myself for battle. I was weak, and it showed in both my spiritual and physical life.

Then one day, I reached my breaking point. I knew I couldn't continue living on the fringes of faith. I decided to immerse myself in God's Word, to truly believe His promises, and to walk in the victory He had already secured for me. As I grew spiritually stronger, my mindset changed. I wasn't fighting alone anymore—I was fighting with God's power. The weight of fear and defeat lifted. I was no longer spiritually starving. I was thriving.

Shaping Bodies & Hearts: Training for Victory

Athletes don't step into the competition unprepared. They train, they discipline themselves, and they develop a victorious mindset long before the race begins. Faith requires the same preparation. If we aren't feeding on the Word, surrounding ourselves with encouragement, and putting in the work, we will feel weak and defeated.

Shaping Bodies: Victory Stance & Strength Training

This movement reflects strength, confidence, and the victorious life we have in Christ. As you move with purpose, let your body mirror the truth that you are more than a conqueror through Him.

Exercise: Victory Pose with Knee Lifts

- Stand tall, holding a weight overhead with both hands, arms fully extended.
- Alternate lifting your knees, one at a time, for 30 seconds to 1 minute.
- Keep your posture strong, shoulders relaxed, core engaged, and back straight.

- Speak **Romans 8:37** aloud as you move: "In all these things we are more than conquerors through Him who loved us."
- **Optional Challenge:** Use a heavier weight and bring it down toward your lifted knee each time. This adds intensity and works your core and upper body more deeply.

Let this exercise become your physical declaration of victory—strong, steady, and full of faith.

Shaping Hearts: Walking in Victory

Declare God's Truth Daily – Say, "I am more than a conqueror through Christ."

Replace Fear with Faith – Identify one area where you've felt defeated and surrender it to God.

Equip Yourself – Read **Romans 8** and meditate on the promises of victory in Christ.

Encourage Someone Else – Victory is not just for you—help someone else claim their identity in Christ.

Dig Deeper

Each morning, stand tall in your Victory Pose with knee lifts and declare Romans 8:37: "In all these things we are more than conquerors through Him who loved us." As you move, reflect on where God is helping you walk in victory. Use the space below to write down a breakthrough, a scripture that stood out, or a moment of strength you experienced today.

Reflection & Prayer

Heavenly Father, thank You for securing my victory through Jesus Christ. Help me to walk in confidence, knowing that I am more than a conqueror. Strengthen my faith, my body, and my spirit so that I may stand firm against every challenge. I claim victory today and every day in Your name. Amen.

My Reflections & Prayer Notes:

_____
_____
_____
_____
_____
_____
_____
_____
_____
_____
_____
_____
_____

Day 7: Faith in Action

Scripture Focus: "Faith by itself, if it is not accompanied by action, is dead." (James 2:17 NIV)

Faith in Motion: Trying or Training?

Faith is more than believing—it's about doing. Just like a workout routine won't strengthen your body unless you actively engage in it, faith won't grow unless you put it into practice. Faith requires action.

For a long time, I thought trying was enough. I would try to pray more, try to read my Bible consistently, try to trust God in difficult moments. But I wasn't seeing change because I was simply trying; I wasn't truly training.

One day, I realized that spiritual growth works the same way as physical training. You don't just "try" to run a marathon; you train daily so that when race day comes, you're prepared. That day, I committed to training my faith—not just believing in God but actively walking in obedience. I started making faith-filled decisions, speaking God's Word over my circumstances, and stepping out of my comfort zone to serve others.

Faith in action transforms not just our lives, but the lives of those around us. When we apply what we believe, we become living testimonies of God's power.

Shaping Bodies & Hearts: Training for Spiritual Strength

In fitness, training is the key to transformation. You don't get stronger by thinking about exercising; you get stronger by moving, lifting, stretching, and pushing past limitations. Similarly, in faith, action is required. When we step out in obedience, even when we don't feel ready, God meets us with His strength.

Shaping Bodies: Step-Up Challenge

Stepping up physically is a great reminder of what it means to step out in faith. It activates your legs, improves balance, and builds strength—just like obedience builds spiritual courage.

Exercise: Step-Ups

- Use a sturdy bench, step, or low platform.
- Step up with your right foot, then bring your left foot up to meet it.
- Step down with your right foot, then your left.
- Continue alternating sides for 1 minute.
- **Optional Challenge:** Hold a pair of light to moderate weights as you step to increase strength and coordination.

As you step up, visualize stepping into God's calling—even when it feels uncertain. Each step is a declaration of trust, faith, and forward movement.

Shaping Hearts: Applying Your Faith Daily

Make One Faith-Based Decision Today – Whether it's trusting God in a difficult moment, praying for someone, or speaking life over a challenge—act in faith.

Serve Someone – Faith grows when we step beyond ourselves to bless others.

Speak Scripture Over Your Circumstances – Declare God's promises over your life.

Step Out of Your Comfort Zone – Take one action that requires trusting God completely.

Dig Deeper

Throughout this week, be mindful of both your physical and spiritual posture. Stand tall in faith and fitness, trusting that God is leading you in the right direction.

Reflection & Prayer

Heavenly Father, help me to put my faith into action daily. I don't want to just believe—I want to walk boldly in obedience. Strengthen me to trust You, to step out even when it's hard, and to live a life that reflects Your love and power. Amen.

My Reflections & Prayer Notes:

Week 2: Realignment and Renewal

Scripture Focus:
"Trust in the Lord with all your heart; do not depend on your own understanding. Seek his will in all you do, and he will show you which path to take." (Proverbs 3:5-6)

Weekly Focus:
This week is about coming into alignment—physically, emotionally, and spiritually. Let God re-center your heart and renew your purpose as you make space for His guidance in every area of your life.

Weekly Prayer:
Father, help me to let go of my own understanding and follow Your leading. Align my spirit, mind, and body with Your will. Renew me from the inside out. Amen.

Day 8: Pressing On

Scripture Focus: "I press on toward the goal to win the prize for which God has called me heavenward in Christ Jesus." (Philippians 3:14 NIV)

Faith in Motion: Running the Right Race

Life is filled with obstacles, setbacks, and challenges. But our faith journey is not about avoiding struggles; it's about persevering through them. When we press on, we develop spiritual endurance and experience the joy of finishing strong in Christ.

For years, I was focused on my own goals, working hard, striving for achievement, and pushing myself to my limits. But no matter how much I accomplished, I felt empty. I was running a race, but it was for my own glory, not God's.

One day, God shifted my perspective. I realized that true endurance isn't about speed or competition—it's about faithfully staying the course with God. Just like training for a marathon, pressing on in faith requires consistency, perseverance, and trust. It's not about how fast we get there, but about staying committed to the path God has set before us.

Shaping Bodies & Hearts: Endurance Training

In fitness, endurance training is what builds stamina and strength over time. You don't wake up one day and run a marathon without preparation. It takes small, daily efforts that eventually lead to big results. Similarly, our spiritual endurance grows when we keep pressing forward in faith, even when it's difficult.

Shaping Bodies: Endurance Circuit Workout

Just like faith, physical endurance takes practice, persistence, and a willingness to keep going–especially when things get tough. This circuit challenges your whole body while reminding you to press forward with purpose.

Exercise: Endurance Circuit

- **Step-Ups (1 minute):** Step up and down on a sturdy platform, alternating legs. Build strength and focus with each repetition.
- **Victory Stance Knee Drive with Weight (30 seconds to 1 minute):** Hold a weight overhead, alternate knee lifts. Optional: bring the weight down toward your knee for added challenge.
- **Plank Hold (30 seconds to 1 minute):** Maintain a strong, stable plank–engage your core, breathe deeply, and stay focused.

Repeat this circuit 2-3 times, increasing intensity as you are able.

As you move through each round, remind yourself: *Endurance is built step by step. With each movement, you're becoming stronger in body and more steadfast in faith.*

Shaping Hearts: Building Perseverance

Reflect on Past Victories – Think about times when God carried you through hardships.

Commit to Faith-Filled Endurance – When challenges come, choose to trust God rather than giving up.

Encourage Someone Else – Uplift a friend who may be struggling to press on in their faith journey.

Pray for Renewed Strength – Ask God to give you perseverance to stay the course.

Dig Deeper

Each day, push yourself to go one step further, whether in your workout, your faith, or your daily challenges. Keep a journal of how God strengthens you when you choose to press on.

Reflection & Prayer

Heavenly Father, thank You for giving me the strength to press on. Help me to remain steadfast in my faith, even when the road is difficult. Teach me to rely on You for endurance and to run my race with perseverance. I trust that You will carry me to the finish line. Amen.

My Reflections & Prayer Notes:

Day 9: Getting Into Alignment

Scripture Focus: "Trust in the Lord with all your heart and lean not on your own understanding; in all your ways submit to him, and he will make your paths straight." (Proverbs 3:5-6 NIV)

Faith in Motion: Finding Alignment

Alignment is crucial—both in our spiritual walk and in our physical health. When we are properly aligned, we move efficiently, live pain-free, and operate according to God's design. But when we are out of alignment, everything feels off—we struggle more, face unnecessary resistance, and feel disconnected from God's purpose for our lives.

There was a time when I ignored the signs that my body was out of alignment. I pushed through workouts despite nagging pain, telling myself I was just being strong. But one day, my body had enough—I suffered an injury that forced me to stop everything. That pause made me realize how much I had neglected proper form and balance, and it reminded me how easy it is to become misaligned in our faith as well.

Just as I needed a physical reset, I needed a spiritual alignment check. Was I truly trusting God, or was I forcing my own way? Was I listening to His guidance, or pushing through on my own strength? When I finally realigned myself with God's Word and surrendered control, everything changed. I found clarity, strength, and peace in knowing I was walking in step with Him.

Shaping Bodies & Hearts: Proper Alignment Brings Strength

In fitness, good posture and alignment prevent injury and help us move efficiently. If our form is off, we waste energy and strain muscles unnecessarily. In our faith, when we align ourselves with God's truth, we experience His peace and purpose.

Shaping Bodies: Posture & Core Alignment

This routine helps improve posture and strengthen the core—reminding us that just as our bodies need proper alignment, so do our hearts and minds in Christ.

Wall Squat Hold:

- Stand with your back flat against a wall, feet shoulder-width apart, and about two feet away from the wall.
- Slowly slide down the wall until your knees are bent at a 90-degree angle (or as low as you can go comfortably).

- Keep your back and head pressed against the wall.
- **Hold this position for 30–60 seconds**, engaging your core and breathing deeply.

As you hold and slide, reflect on areas where God may be calling you to stand firm in faith or adjust your spiritual posture to better align with His truth.

Shaping Hearts: Aligning with God's Will

Assess Your Alignment – Are your daily habits reflecting trust in God, or are you leaning on your own strength?

Surrender Control – Ask God to reveal areas where you need to let go and realign with His will.

Commit to Daily Check-Ins – Just as you adjust your posture throughout the day, take moments to check your spiritual alignment through prayer and scripture.

Seek Accountability – Surround yourself with people who encourage you to stay aligned with God's truth.

Dig Deeper

As you go about your day, pay attention to your posture—both physically and spiritually. When you feel tension, fatigue, or resistance, pause and realign. Take a deep breath, stand tall in God's truth, and ask Him to straighten any crooked paths. Use the space below to reflect on one area where He may be calling you to adjust your focus, release control, or trust Him more fully.

Reflection & Prayer

Heavenly Father, I desire to be in full alignment with Your will. Help me to trust You completely and to walk the path You have set before me. Correct my posture when I lean on my own understanding and keep me standing firm in Your truth. Amen.

My Reflections & Prayer Notes:

_____
_____
_____
_____
_____
_____
_____
_____
_____
_____
_____
_____
_____
_____
_____
_____

Day 10: A Well-Watered Garden

Scripture Focus: "The Lord will guide you always; He will satisfy your needs in a sun-scorched land and will strengthen your frame. You will be like a well-watered garden, like a spring whose waters never fail." (Isaiah 58:11 NIV)

Faith in Motion: Finding Spiritual Nourishment

Our faith, much like a garden, requires consistent care and nourishment. Without water, plants wither, roots weaken, and growth is stunted. In the same way, when we neglect our spiritual health, we become dry, weary, and disconnected from the life-giving presence of God. But when we stay rooted in Him, we flourish.

I remember a time when I felt spiritually drained. I was pouring out—serving, leading, and taking care of others—but I wasn't taking the time to refill my own well. Just like a plant that hadn't received rain for weeks, I started to feel weak, my joy diminished, and my energy ran low.

One day, I realized that I needed to water my own soul before I could pour into others. I carved out time for quiet moments with God, prayer, and His Word. It wasn't an instant transformation, but over time, I felt renewed, strengthened, and deeply rooted in Him again. Just as a garden thrives when tended to, so does our faith when we stay connected to our source of living water—Jesus.

Shaping Bodies & Hearts: Hydration and Renewal

In fitness, hydration is key to sustaining energy and performance. When we don't drink enough water, we experience fatigue, muscle cramps, and decreased endurance. Likewise, spiritually, we must stay filled with God's presence to remain strong.

Shaping Bodies: Hydration & Restoration Routine

Hydration isn't just about drinking water—it's about intentionally caring for your body so you can function at your best. Just like we need living water for our souls, our bodies need physical hydration to thrive.

Hydration & Recovery Tips:

- **Drink Water Intentionally:** Carry a water bottle with you and set hydration goals throughout the day. A general guideline is to drink half your body weight in ounces of water daily. Increase your intake on workout days or when spending more time outdoors.

- **Support Electrolytes Naturally:** When doing intense workouts or sweating more than usual, consider adding electrolytes. A simple option is placing a few granules of Celtic sea salt on your tongue before or after a workout. This can help replenish essential minerals.
- **Stretch & Breathe:** After exercising, gently stretch your muscles and take slow, deep breaths to help your body recover.
- **Rest & Meditate:** Spend 5 minutes in God's presence. Read a scripture, worship quietly, or simply be still and reflect on His promises.

As you hydrate your body, don't forget to hydrate your soul—with prayer, scripture, and moments of stillness in God's presence.

Shaping Hearts: Staying Spiritually Nourished

Daily Watering – Read at least one passage of scripture daily to refresh your spirit.

Prayer Time – Set aside intentional time to talk to God and refill your soul.

Community Growth – Stay connected with other believers who will encourage and water your faith.

Remove the Weeds – Identify distractions or negative influences that may be stunting your spiritual growth and remove them.

Dig Deeper

Be intentional about staying hydrated physically and spiritually. Drink plenty of water and spend daily time soaking in God's Word, allowing Him to refresh and renew you.

Reflection & Prayer

Heavenly Father, I desire to be like a well-watered garden, thriving in Your presence. Help me to stay nourished by Your Word and filled with Your living water. Let my life be a reflection of Your abundant love and care. Amen.

My Reflections & Prayer Notes:

_____
_____
_____
_____
_____
_____
_____
_____
_____
_____
_____

Day 11: Identity & Preventing Identity Theft

Scripture Focus: "But you are a chosen people, a royal priesthood, a holy nation, God's special possession, that you may declare the praises of him who called you out of darkness into his wonderful light." (1 Peter 2:9 NIV)

Faith in Motion: Finding Our True Identity in Christ

There was a time in my life when I let others define who I was. I sought validation through achievements, approval, and worldly success. For several years, I ran races—and won 50 first-place trophies, whether in my age group or as the overall winner. But I wasn't running for joy or health—I was running for approval. Each trophy gave me a temporary high, but deep down, I still felt insecure and empty.

Our identity in Christ is one of the most powerful truths we can embrace. Yet, the enemy works tirelessly to distort, deceive, and steal that truth from us. He wants us to believe we are unworthy, weak, and defeated. But God calls us chosen, loved, and victorious.

It wasn't until I dug into God's Word that I realized who I truly was—a daughter of the King, created with a divine purpose. The enemy had tried to steal my identity by whispering lies: "You're not good enough. You're not strong enough. You don't matter." But when I began declaring God's truth over my life, those lies lost their power. I reclaimed my identity in Christ, and in doing so, I found true confidence, strength, and peace.

Shaping Bodies & Hearts: Strength in Identity

In fitness, knowing your starting point and goals is crucial. If you train with the wrong mindset, thinking you're too weak or incapable, you will struggle to make progress. Similarly, in faith, if we don't understand who we are in Christ, we will walk in defeat rather than victory.

Shaping Bodies: Confidence & Core Strength Routine

Just as embracing your identity in Christ builds spiritual confidence, strengthening your core builds physical confidence and stability. Today's movement encourages both.

Exercise: Stability Ball Crunches

- Sit on a stability ball with feet flat on the floor and hands behind your head.
- Walk your feet forward slightly and roll down until your lower back rests on the ball.

- Engage your core and lift your upper body into a crunch.
- Lower slowly with control.
- Optional Challenge: Hold a light weight at your chest or extended overhead for added resistance.
- Perform 10–15 repetitions.

As you crunch, repeat: *"I am chosen. I am strong. I am God's masterpiece."*

Let each movement remind you that your strength flows from your identity in Christ—unshakable and true.

Shaping Hearts: Guarding Your Identity

Recognize the Lies – Identify negative thoughts that do not align with God's Word.

Replace with Truth – Speak scriptures over yourself, like **1 Peter 2:9** and **Romans 8:37**.

Walk in Confidence – Each day, remind yourself that you are loved, chosen, and victorious in Christ.

Encourage Others – Speak life into someone else's identity, helping them reclaim their worth in God.

Dig Deeper

Each day, declare a scripture-based affirmation over your life. Write it down, speak it out loud, and walk in the confidence of who God created you to be!

Reflection & Prayer

Heavenly Father, thank You for calling me Your own. Help me to stand firm in my identity and resist the enemy's lies. I declare that I am chosen, loved, and victorious in Christ. Let my confidence rest not in my strength but in Your truth. Amen.

My Reflections & Prayer Notes:

_____
_____
_____
_____
_____
_____
_____
_____
_____
_____
_____
_____
_____
_____
_____
_____
_____

Day 12: Guard Your Heart

Scripture Focus: "Above all else, guard your heart, for everything you do flows from it." (Proverbs 4:23 NIV)

Faith in Motion: Learning to Protect My Heart

Our hearts are at the center of everything we do—our thoughts, emotions, and actions all flow from this core. That's why God instructs us to guard our hearts diligently. Just as we protect our physical health from harm, we must also be intentional in protecting our spiritual health from distractions, negative influences, and anything that draws us away from God's truth.

There was a season in my life when I felt pulled in many directions—juggling responsibilities, listening to too many voices, and letting worries take up space in my heart. I didn't even realize how much these distractions were weighing me down until I made a conscious effort to refocus on God.

I began filtering what I allowed into my mind and heart. Instead of dwelling on negative thoughts, I replaced them with scripture. I spent more time in prayer and worship, seeking God's presence daily. Over time, I noticed a shift—I felt lighter, more peaceful, and more in tune with God's voice. Guarding my heart wasn't about closing myself off, but about being intentional with what I allowed in.

Shaping Bodies & Hearts: Strengthening the Heart

In fitness, cardiovascular health is key to overall strength and endurance. The stronger our hearts, the more energy and resilience we have. In the same way, when our spiritual hearts are strong, we can resist temptation, stay firm in our faith, and walk boldly in God's truth.

Shaping Bodies: Heart-Strengthening Kettlebell Routine

Just as we guard our spiritual hearts, we also strengthen our physical hearts through intentional movement. This full-body cardio routine helps boost endurance and heart health while reminding you to stay strong in spirit.

Exercise: Kettlebell Swing Circuit

Perform each swing for **30 seconds to 1 minute**, resting briefly between moves.
If you don't have a kettlebell, use a single dumbbell instead.

- **Double Arm Swing:** Hold the kettlebell or dumbbell with both hands, swing it back between your legs, then drive your hips forward to swing it to chest height.
- **Alternate Arm Swing:** Swing with one arm at a time, switching hands at the top of each swing.

- **High Swing:** Swing the weight just above shoulder height for increased intensity.
- **Squat Swing:** Add a deep squat before each swing to engage the glutes and legs even more.

Keep your core engaged and breathe rhythmically. Focus on power from the hips, not the arms.

As your heart rate rises, **pray for God to protect and strengthen your spiritual heart**. Ask Him to help you stay alert, pure, and firmly rooted in His truth.

Shaping Hearts: Protecting Your Heart Daily

Filter What You Consume – Be mindful of the media, conversations, and relationships you allow into your life.

Strengthen Your Faith Daily – Spend time in God's Word, prayer, and worship.

Surround Yourself with Encouragement – Seek friendships that uplift and challenge you spiritually.

Let Go of Toxic Influences – Identify anything that is pulling you away from God's best and remove it from your life.

Dig Deeper

Begin each day by checking what you're allowing into your heart. Choose to replace negativity with God's truth and commit to strengthening both your physical and spiritual heart with intention.

Reflection & Prayer

Heavenly Father, help me to guard my heart against anything that does not align with Your truth. Strengthen me to walk in wisdom, protect my faith, and surround myself with what is good and life-giving. Let my heart be fully devoted to You. Amen.

My Reflections & Prayer Notes:

_____
_____
_____
_____
_____
_____
_____
_____
_____
_____
_____
_____
_____
_____
_____
_____

Day 13: Honoring God with the Body

Scripture Focus: "Do you not know that your bodies are temples of the Holy Spirit, who is in you, whom you have received from God? You are not your own; you were bought at a price. Therefore, honor God with your bodies." (1 Corinthians 6:19-20 NIV)

Faith in Motion: Shifting My Focus to Glorifying God

God created our bodies with intention and purpose—not merely as physical vessels, but as sacred spaces where His Spirit dwells. Honoring Him with our bodies means caring for them, respecting them, and using them as instruments of worship. Just as we're called to steward our time, gifts, and resources, we are also called to steward our health for His glory.

In the early years of my fitness journey, my motivation was rooted in appearance and performance—reaching a goal weight, toning muscles, and chasing after trophies. I was driven by personal achievement, not eternal purpose. No matter how many milestones I reached, something always felt missing.

Everything changed when I fully surrendered my life to Christ. I realized my workouts weren't just about physical transformation—they were opportunities to glorify God. What once felt like striving became surrender. Each class I taught and each movement I practiced became a worship session unto the Lord. I stopped training for perfection and started moving in gratitude, discipline, and reverence for the body God had entrusted to me.

Shaping Bodies & Hearts: Stewardship of the Body

Caring for our bodies is not about vanity or obsession; it's about obedience and gratitude. Just as we take care of our spiritual health through prayer and scripture, we honor God by keeping our bodies strong, nourished, and energized for His purpose.

Shaping Bodies: Full-Body Strength & Balance Workout

This routine symbolizes balance—between faith and fitness, discipline and grace. As you move, focus on maintaining control and staying grounded, both physically and spiritually.

Exercise: Alternate Reverse Lunges with Biceps Curl

- Hold a pair of weights at your sides.
- Step your right foot back into a lunge, bending both knees to 90 degrees.
- As you return to standing, curl the weights toward your shoulders.
- Alternate legs and repeat for **10-12 reps per side**.
- Move with purpose, keeping your core engaged and maintaining an upright posture.

This exercise improves **balance, coordination, and total-body strength**, reminding you that strength in motion is rooted in stability and grace.

As you lunge and lift, **pray over your body—thanking God for your health, ability, and the strength He provides each day.**

Shaping Hearts: Honoring God Through Daily Choices

True transformation happens when we honor God with our everyday decisions – how we move, rest, speak, and nourish ourselves.

Fuel Your Body Well – Choose foods that nourish and energize, remembering that your body is a temple of the Holy Spirit.

Move with Purpose – Exercise not out of guilt, but as a celebration of what your body can do—strengthened by God for His purpose.

Rest as Worship – Prioritize rest and recovery, recognizing that God calls us to rhythms of both work and renewal.

Speak Life Over Your Body – Reject negative self-talk and declare God's truth: "*I am fearfully and wonderfully made*" (Psalm 139:14).

Pray with Posture – Try sitting on a stability ball during your Bible reading or prayer time. It gently engages your core, improves posture, and reminds you to stay spiritually and physically balanced throughout the day.

Each choice you make can be an act of worship. Let your body and heart reflect the love and discipline of Christ.

Dig Deeper

Today, choose one intentional way to honor God with your body—through movement, nourishment, rest, or simply a word of gratitude. Let that act be a quiet offering of worship to the One who created you with purpose.

Reflection & Prayer

Heavenly Father, thank You for creating my body as a temple for Your Spirit. Help me to steward my health well, making choices that honor You. May my movements be worship, my strength be used for Your glory, and my heart remain focused on serving You. Amen.

My Reflections & Prayer Notes:

_____
_____
_____
_____
_____
_____
_____
_____
_____
_____
_____
_____
_____
_____
_____
_____

Day 14: Where Faith Meets Fitness

Scripture Focus: "Love the Lord your God with all your heart and with all your soul and with all your strength." (Deuteronomy 6:5 NIV)

Faith in Motion: A Heart Strengthened by Faith

Faith and fitness are deeply connected. Just as we nurture our spiritual health through prayer, worship, and time in God's Word, we must also take care of our physical health. When we approach fitness as an act of worship, it shifts from being a chore to a way to honor God with our bodies and grow in strength—physically and spiritually.

I know firsthand how vital it is to take care of the heart. I was born with three holes in my heart, a congenital heart defect that required two open-heart surgeries, the first in November 1987 and the second in September 2007. Through it all, God sustained me, not just physically, but spiritually, strengthening me for the calling He placed on my life.

I thank God every day for saving me twice—once through surgery and ultimately through His grace. My journey has deepened my understanding of how interconnected our spiritual and physical well-being truly are. Just as we must care for our physical hearts with movement, nourishment, and rest, we must also nurture our spiritual hearts with prayer, worship, and trust in God's promises.

Shaping Bodies & Hearts: Strengthening the Heart

A strong heart is essential for endurance, whether in exercise or faith. Just as we engage in cardio training to build a healthy heart, we must also train our spiritual hearts to stay strong in the Lord.

Shaping Bodies: Heart-Focused Workout

This workout is designed to support cardiovascular health and build endurance—just as your faith walk requires perseverance, strength, and gratitude. Each movement is a reminder that every heartbeat is a gift from God.

Exercise: Step-Ups (2 minutes):
Use a sturdy step or bench. Step up with your right foot, then your left, and step back down. Continue alternating. *To increase the challenge, hold light weights or move at a brisk pace.*

Exercise: Rebounder or Low-Impact Cardio (1 minute):
If you have a rebounder, gently bounce to activate circulation and lift your energy. If not, do low-impact cardio such as side steps or low-impact jumping jacks.

Exercise: Overhead Knee Drives (1 minute):
Hold a weight overhead. Alternate lifting knees toward your chest, driving with control.
For added intensity, bring the weight down toward your knee as you lift.

As you move, lift your heart in gratitude. **Thank God for every beat, every breath, and the strength to keep moving forward in faith.**

Shaping Hearts: Strengthening Your Faith Daily

Pray for Your Physical & Spiritual Heart: Ask God to strengthen you inside and out.

Move with Purpose: View physical activity as an act of worship and gratitude.

Fuel Your Body & Soul: Nourish yourself with both healthy food and God's Word.

Trust in God's Strength: When challenges come, rely on Him for endurance.

Dig Deeper

As you move today, reflect on how God has strengthened your heart—through healing, through grace, and through every breath He gives. If you feel led, jot down a moment when He carried you through and gave you endurance to keep going.

Reflection & Prayer

Lord, thank You for the gift of life and the bodies You've given us. Help us honor You through movement and faith, treating each breath as a gift. Let our workouts be worship, strengthening body and spirit. When we're weak, be our strength. Renew our hearts and align us with Your purpose. We give our health and faith to You. May we seek You first in all we do. Amen.

My Reflections & Prayer Notes:

_____
_____
_____
_____
_____
_____
_____
_____
_____
_____
_____
_____
_____
_____

Week 3: Drawing Closer to God

Scripture Focus:
"Draw near to God, and He will draw near to you." (James 4:8 NKJV)

Weekly Focus:
As you continue, press into a deeper relationship with God. Build consistency in your spiritual habits and allow your hunger for His Word to grow. Let your mornings, your mindset, and your movement be centered around His presence.

Weekly Prayer:
God, draw me closer to You this week. Let my heart be stirred for more of Your Word, Your truth, and Your love. Deepen my desire to know You intimately. Amen.

Day 15: Drawing Closer to God

Scripture Focus: "Draw close to God and He will draw close to you." (James 4:8 NKJV)

Faith in Motion: Chasing After God

Our relationship with God is like any other relationship—it grows through time, intentionality, and consistent pursuit. Just as an athlete trains daily to improve, our faith strengthens when we actively seek God. He invites us to draw near, and when we do, He meets us with His presence, wisdom, and peace.

Before I fully surrendered my heart to Christ, I believed faith was mostly about attending church and turning to God in times of crisis. But everything changed when I gave Him my whole heart. That's when I became a God chaser—someone who didn't just believe but passionately pursued a deeper relationship with Him.

Surrounding myself with others who were hungry for God sparked something new in me. Their devotion stirred a longing in my soul, and I committed to making God the center of my daily life. I began setting aside intentional time for prayer, worship, and reading His Word—not out of duty, but desire. The more I chased after Him, the more I experienced His nearness.

God was no longer someone I reached for in emergencies—He became my daily strength, my faithful guide, and the source of my deepest joy.

Shaping Bodies & Hearts: Training with Purpose

Athletes don't train sporadically if they want to succeed—they follow a disciplined routine. Likewise, spiritual growth requires consistency. The more we invest in our faith, the deeper our relationship with God becomes.

Shaping Bodies: Spiritual Consistency

This workout mirrors spiritual consistency—moving with purpose, strength, and rhythm. As you move, think about how your physical discipline can reflect your daily walk with Christ.

Exercise: Rhythmic Training Routine

- **Kettlebell or Dumbbell Swings (30 seconds to 1 minute):** Swing the weight with controlled power, engaging your hips and core.
  Let the rhythm of the movement remind you of spiritual momentum and breakthrough.
- **Squats (15 reps):** Stand with feet shoulder-width apart and lower into a squat. Rise with strength.

Builds physical and spiritual stability—rooted in God's truth.
- **Plank Hold (30 seconds to 1 minute):** Keep your body in a straight line from head to heels, engaging your core.
Just like spending quiet time with God, this strengthens your foundation from within.

Shaping Hearts: Pursuing God Daily

Prioritize Time with Him – Set a designated time for prayer and Bible study each day.

Eliminate Distractions – Identify what may be keeping you from deeper intimacy with God and create boundaries.

Surround Yourself with Faith-Filled People – Walk alongside those who encourage you to grow spiritually.

Seek God in Everything – Invite Him into your daily routines—your work, workouts, and conversations.

Dig Deeper

Just as your body responds to consistent movement, your spirit grows stronger through steady time with God. Choose a moment today to pause, seek His presence, and let Him draw near. Let this be a sacred rhythm in your walk of faith.

Reflection & Prayer

Heavenly Father, help me seek You daily with passion and discipline. Strengthen my faith, align my heart with Your will, and deepen our relationship. May my pursuit of You be as intentional as caring for my body, bringing You honor in all I do. Amen.

My Reflections & Prayer Notes:

_____
_____
_____
_____
_____
_____
_____
_____
_____
_____
_____
_____
_____
_____
_____
_____
_____

Day 16: My Morning Wake-Up Call

Scripture Focus: "My voice You shall hear in the morning, O Lord; In the morning I will direct it to you, and I will look up." (Psalm 5:3 NKJV)

Faith in Motion: Meeting God at the Start of the Day

For as long as I can remember, I have been an early riser. My internal clock says, "Get up, get going, and get something done!" Though there are mornings when I would love to linger a little longer in bed, my spirit urges me to rise and meet with the Father. My true morning wake-up call isn't the sound of an alarm clock—it's the prompting of God's presence, calling me into sacred time with Him.

Spending my mornings with God prepares me for the day ahead. It refuels my spirit, quiets my heart, and sets the foundation for everything that follows. Before the distractions of the day begin, before responsibilities pile up, I seek Him in the stillness, knowing that He is already waiting for me.

One of my favorite ways to meet with God is outdoors. The fresh air, the vibrant colors of nature, and the quiet of the early morning provide the perfect setting to hear His voice. Watching the sunrise reminds me that every day is a gift—an opportunity to glorify Him in all that I do.

Shaping Bodies & Hearts: Morning Movement & Mindset

Just as we need to wake up our bodies with movement, we need to wake up our spirits with God's truth. A strong morning routine—both physically and spiritually—sets the tone for the day ahead. Just as stretching and exercise prepare our muscles for activity, prayer and time in God's Word prepare our hearts to walk in His purpose.

Shaping Bodies: Aligned with God's Purpose

This gentle routine awakens the body and energizes the spirit, helping you start the day aligned with God's peace and purpose.

Exercise: Morning Mobility & Stability Routine

- **Standing Side Stretch (30 seconds per side):** Reach one arm overhead and gently lean to the opposite side. Feel the lengthening through your side body as you breathe deeply and open your heart to God's presence.
- **Deep Breathing with Arm Raises (1 minute):** Inhale deeply while raising your arms overhead, then exhale

slowly as you lower them. Let each breath remind you of God's peace and provision.
- **Cat/Cow Exercise (1 minute):**
Begin on your hands and knees in a tabletop position.
    - **Inhale** as you arch your back, lifting your head and tailbone (Cow).
    - **Exhale** as you round your spine, tucking your chin and tailbone (Cat).
    Breathe slowly, releasing tension and gently aligning your spine.

As you move through this routine, thank God for the gift of a new day and invite Him to align your heart, mind, and body for His purpose.

Shaping Hearts: Setting the Tone for the Day

Seek God First – Begin your day with prayer and scripture before engaging with the outside world.

Find Your Sanctuary – Whether it's a quiet room or an outdoor space, create a place where you can meet with God.

Start with Gratitude – Acknowledge God's blessings before focusing on daily tasks.

Meditate on His Promises – Carry a scripture with you throughout the day to keep your heart aligned with His truth.

Dig Deeper

As the sun rises, let your spirit rise to meet God. Step into stillness, breathe deeply, and listen for His voice. Whether indoors or out, create a sacred space where you start your day aligned with His presence.

Reflection & Prayer

Heavenly Father, thank You for a new day. Help me seek You first, before distractions come. Strengthen my heart, mind, and body to walk in Your will. May my morning begin with worship, gratitude, and purpose. Amen.

My Reflections & Prayer Notes:

_____
_____
_____
_____
_____
_____
_____
_____
_____
_____
_____

Day 17: Devouring the Word

Scripture Focus: "Man shall not live on bread alone, but on every word that comes from the mouth of God." (Matthew 4:4 NIV)

Faith in Motion: Learning to Hunger for God's Word

Our bodies rely on food for nourishment, energy, and growth. Without it, we become weak, fatigued, and unable to function at our best. The same is true for our spiritual lives—if we neglect the Word of God, our faith becomes malnourished, leaving us spiritually weak and disconnected from Him.

There was a time in my life when I viewed reading the Bible as something I should do rather than something I needed to do. It felt more like a habit to check off my list rather than a source of life and strength. But one day, everything changed.

I began truly devouring the Word—not just reading it, but soaking it in, reflecting on it, and letting it transform my heart and mind. The more I consumed, the hungrier I became. Just as physical food fuels our bodies, I realized that scripture was fueling my soul, equipping me with everything I needed for the challenges ahead. I no longer read it out of obligation—I read it because I craved it.

Shaping Bodies & Hearts: Fueling the Body and Spirit

In fitness, proper nutrition is essential. Without the right food, we feel drained, sluggish, and unable to perform at our best. Likewise, if we aren't regularly feeding on God's Word, we become spiritually depleted.

Shaping Bodies: Strength & Nourishment Routine

This exercise reminds us that just as we feed our bodies with nutritious food, we must also feed our faith with God's Word and consistent discipline.

Exercise: Squat to Shoulder Press (15 reps)

- Stand with feet shoulder-width apart, holding dumbbells at shoulder height.
- Lower into a squat, keeping your chest lifted and knees behind your toes.
- Rise to standing, pressing the dumbbells overhead.
- Return the weights to shoulder level and repeat. *This full-body movement builds strength and control—just like nourishing your faith with Scripture strengthens your spiritual foundation.*

Shaping Hearts: Feeding on the Word Daily

Set a Scripture Schedule – Plan daily Bible reading just like you would plan meals.

Meditate on God's Word – Take time to reflect on scripture rather than rushing through it.

Memorize Key Verses – Hide God's Word in your heart so you can recall it in times of need.

Share Scripture with Others – Just as we share meals, share God's Word to encourage someone else.

Dig Deeper

Just as your body needs regular nourishment, so does your soul. Open God's Word today, even if just one verse, and let it fill you with strength. Reflect on how it fuels your spirit and share it with someone who may need spiritual encouragement.

Reflection & Prayer

Heavenly Father, thank You for the nourishment of Your Word. Help me to hunger for it daily and rely on it as my source of strength. Just as my body needs food to thrive, my spirit needs Your truth to sustain me. Fill me with wisdom, renew my heart, and strengthen my faith as I devour Your Word. Amen.

My Reflections & Prayer Notes:

Day 18: Keeping Your Head Over Your Heart

Scripture Focus: "Trust in the Lord with all your heart and lean not on your own understanding; in all your ways submit to him, and he will make your paths straight." (Proverbs 3:5-6 NIV)

Faith in Motion: A Heart in Alignment

Life is full of moments that test our emotions and challenge our thinking. It's easy to let feelings dictate our actions, but God calls us to align our hearts with His truth. Just as good posture and proper form protect us during exercise, spiritual alignment protects us in our daily walk. When emotions rise up—fear, frustration, or discouragement—we must choose to anchor ourselves in God's wisdom instead of letting feelings take the lead.

Keeping our "head over our heart" means allowing God's Word to steady our thoughts, guide our decisions, and shape our responses. Just as a strong core keeps the body stable, God's truth keeps our spirit steady. When we stay aligned with Him, we not only prevent injury from poor decisions but also build endurance to stand firm in faith no matter what challenges come our way.

This alignment doesn't happen overnight—it requires daily discipline. Just like we train our bodies through consistent exercise, we train our minds and hearts through consistent time in Scripture and prayer. The more we practice choosing faith over feelings, the stronger our spiritual "muscles" become. With God's Word as our anchor, we can walk in confidence, knowing that our emotions don't have the final say—He does.

Shaping Bodies & Hearts: Proper Alignment Prevents Injury

In fitness, maintaining proper form is crucial. Misalignment can lead to injury, just as misaligned priorities and emotions can lead us down the wrong spiritual path. Keeping your head over your heart means balancing wisdom and emotions, ensuring that faith, not feelings, leads the way.

Shaping Bodies: Core Stability & Balance Routine

This workout focuses on stability and alignment—reminding us to stay grounded in truth and balanced in our walk with God. Just as your core stabilizes your movements, God's Word anchors your spirit.

Exercise: Seated Stability Ball Chest Press with Leg Extension (12–15 reps)

- Sit tall on a stability ball with a dumbbell in each hand, elbows bent at your sides and dumbbells near chest level.
- Engage your core and plant your feet firmly.
- As you press the dumbbells upward toward the ceiling, extend your right leg straight out in front of you.
- Lower the dumbbells back to the starting position and bring your leg down.
- Repeat, alternating legs with each press.
  Keep your core tight, shoulders relaxed, and maintain steady breathing throughout.

Shaping Hearts: Aligning with God's Wisdom

Pause Before Reacting – When emotions rise, take a moment to seek God's wisdom before making decisions.

Anchor Yourself in Scripture – Keep a verse close that reminds you to trust in God's plan over feelings.

Surround Yourself with Wise Counsel – Seek advice from godly mentors who help you stay aligned with truth.

Daily Surrender – Each morning, ask God to guide your heart and mind in perfect alignment with His will.

Dig Deeper

Before you respond to life's challenges, pause and check your alignment—both physically and spiritually. Are your thoughts grounded in truth, or led by emotion? Let God's wisdom steady your steps and guide your posture, inside and out.

Reflection & Prayer

Heavenly Father, help me to keep my head above my heart, aligning my thoughts and emotions with Your truth. Teach me to trust in You rather than relying on my own understanding. May my heart be steadfast, my faith unwavering, and my body strong as I live according to Your wisdom. Amen.

My Reflections & Prayer Notes:

_____
_____
_____
_____
_____
_____
_____
_____

Day 19: The Heart of a Healthy Marriage

Scripture Focus: "Though one may be overpowered, two can defend themselves. A cord of three strands is not quickly broken." (Ecclesiastes 4:12 NIV)

Faith in Motion: Strengthening Our Marriage Through Faith

Marriage is a gift from God, a covenant designed to reflect His love, grace, and unity. But like anything valuable, it requires intentional care, endurance, and a strong foundation in faith. A healthy marriage is not just about compatibility; it's about commitment, selflessness, and keeping Christ at the center.

When I first got married, I quickly learned that love alone wasn't enough to sustain a strong relationship. There were moments of misunderstandings, struggles, and trials—times when my husband and I could have let stress and differences pull us apart. But what held us together was our decision to keep God first.

We learned that a healthy marriage is like fitness training—it takes consistent effort, discipline, and a willingness to grow. Just as our bodies need the right exercises to stay strong, our marriage needed prayer, communication, and trust in God to thrive. By leaning on Him, we found unity, strength, and a deeper love than we ever imagined.

Shaping Bodies & Hearts: Building Strength in Marriage

In fitness, you don't build strength overnight. It takes daily effort, perseverance, and proper conditioning. The same is true in marriage—it requires:

Consistency – Regular time together in prayer and communication.

Endurance – Pushing through difficult moments instead of giving up.

Proper Form – Keeping God at the center rather than relying on our strength.

Shaping Bodies: Partner Strength Workout

This workout reinforces the power of unity, trust, and mutual support—just like in a Christ-centered marriage or close friendship.

Exercise: Partner Squat and Resistance Band Row (30-60 seconds)

- Stand facing your partner, each holding one end of a resistance band.
- Step back to create light tension in the band.
- Simultaneously squat down, then rise while pulling the band toward your torso in a double-arm row.
- Focus on staying in sync and maintaining good form.

Exercise: Medicine Ball Pass (30-60 seconds)

- Stand a few feet apart and toss a weighted medicine ball back and forth.
- Keep your core engaged and movements controlled.

Shaping Hearts: Strengthening Your Marriage Through Faith

Pray Together Daily – Invite God into your marriage through prayer.

Speak Life Over Each Other – Use words that encourage rather than tear down.

Show Grace in Conflict – Forgive quickly and choose unity over division.

Make Time for Growth – Invest in your relationship with intentional time together.

Dig Deeper

Think of one intentional way you can pour into your marriage today—through prayer, encouragement, or simply listening with love. Let your actions mirror Christ's love and strengthen the bond you share.

Reflection & Prayer

Heavenly Father, thank You for the gift of marriage. Help us to build a relationship that honors You, full of love, grace, and strength. Teach us to grow together, to rely on You in every season, and to be an example of Your love to the world. Amen.

My Reflections & Prayer Notes:

_____
_____
_____
_____
_____
_____
_____
_____
_____
_____
_____
_____

Day 20: The Face of Grace

Scripture Focus: "But he said to me, My grace is sufficient for you, for my power is made perfect in weakness.' Therefore, I will boast all the more gladly about my weaknesses, so that Christ's power may rest on me." (2 Corinthians 12:9 NIV)

Faith in Motion: Experiencing God's Grace

Grace is a gift freely given, yet so often we struggle to accept it. We hold onto guilt, shame, and self-doubt, believing we must work harder to earn God's love. But the truth is, His grace is more than enough. It's not about what we do—it's about what Christ has already done.

There was a time in my life when I hit rock bottom. I felt unworthy, ashamed of my mistakes, and convinced that I had fallen too far for God to restore me. But in my lowest moment, God met me with grace—not condemnation, not judgment, just pure, undeserved love.

It was then that I truly saw the face of grace—through the kindness of a friend, the encouragement of scripture, and the still, small voice reminding me: You are forgiven. You are loved. You are mine.

Just like a muscle grows through recovery and rest, our faith is strengthened when we learn to receive God's grace instead of striving on our own.

Shaping Bodies & Hearts: Grace in Movement

In fitness, we often push ourselves hard, expecting perfection. But growth happens in the rest—when muscles repair and rebuild. Similarly, in our faith, we grow the most when we rest in God's grace rather than striving for perfection.

Shaping Bodies: Grace-Filled Pilates Bridge

This gentle Pilates movement focuses on restorative strength and controlled breathing, reminding us that God's grace lifts us and sustains us—especially in our weakest moments.

Exercise: Bridge with Breath & Arm Flow (30-60 seconds)

- Lie on your back with knees bent and feet flat on the floor, hip-width apart.
- Place your arms at your sides.
- Inhale to prepare, then exhale as you press through your heels and lift your hips into a bridge position. At the same time, sweep your arms slowly overhead.
- Inhale as you lower your hips back to the floor and bring your arms back down.

Shaping Hearts: Living in Grace Daily

Let Go of Perfection – Release the need to perform or prove yourself to God.

Speak Grace Over Yourself – Replace self-criticism with words of truth and love.

Extend Grace to Others – Forgive quickly and show kindness, just as Christ does for you.

Rest in God's Presence – Spend time with Him, not striving, just being still and receiving.

Dig Deeper

Let grace be your rhythm today. Release the pressure to be perfect and simply rest in God's love. As you move, breathe deeply, and receive what He freely gives—strength, forgiveness, and peace.

Reflection & Prayer

Heavenly Father, thank You for Your boundless grace. Teach me to accept it fully, to live free from guilt, and to extend grace to others as You have so freely given it to me. Help me to trust in Your strength, not my own, and to find rest in Your love. Amen.

My Reflections & Prayer Notes:

Day 21: Can You Hear Me Now?

Scripture Focus: "My sheep listen to my voice; I know them, and they follow me." (John 10:27)

Faith in Motion: Learning to Listen

In a world filled with distractions, it can be difficult to hear God's voice. We often find ourselves consumed by noise—busyness, social media, opinions of others—drowning out the gentle whisper of the Holy Spirit. Yet, God is always speaking. The question is: Are we listening?

There was a season in my life when I desperately needed to hear from God. I prayed constantly, asking for guidance, but all I felt was silence. I remember sitting in my quiet time one morning, frustrated and wondering if God was even listening. I wanted clear answers, but instead, I was met with stillness.

Then, I realized that hearing God isn't about Him speaking louder—it's about me becoming quieter. When I stopped trying to force an answer and instead sat in His presence with expectation, I began noticing His voice in the smallest moments—in scripture, in conversations, in the gentle peace that settled over my heart. God had been speaking all along; I just needed to be still enough to listen."

I started making space for stillness—turning off distractions, spending time in His Word, and being intentional in prayer. The more I listened, the clearer His voice became. He had been speaking all along; I just needed to be still enough to recognize it.

Shaping Bodies & Hearts: Tuning in to the Body

In fitness, listening to our bodies is crucial. When we ignore signs of exhaustion or injury, we risk burnout or harm. Likewise, when we ignore God's voice, we risk missing His guidance and direction. The key to growth—both spiritually and physically—is learning to tune in.

Shaping Bodies: Mindful Movement Routine

This routine encourages you to slow down, breathe deeply, and create space to hear God—body, mind, and spirit in alignment.

Exercise: Seated Saw with Breath Focus (30-60 seconds)

- Sit tall with legs extended wide, feet flexed, and arms stretched out to the sides.
- Inhale to lengthen your spine.
- Exhale as you twist from the waist and reach your front hand toward the opposite foot, as if "sawing" past your pinky toe.

- Inhale to return to center, then repeat on the other side.

Focus on steady breath and control, releasing tension and inviting God's peace with each movement.

Shaping Hearts: Becoming Attuned to God's Voice

Create Quiet Moments – Set aside daily time to be still before God.

Read His Word Expectantly – Approach scripture with the anticipation of hearing from Him.

Pray with Open Ears – Instead of just talking, take time to listen.

Obey Promptings – When you sense God leading you, step out in faith.

Dig Deeper

Create space today to simply be still. Silence the noise around you, close your eyes, and tune in to the voice of the Shepherd. Even a few quiet moments can shift your heart and open your ears to His guidance.

Reflection & Prayer

Heavenly Father, help me to hear Your voice above the noise of the world. Teach me to quiet my heart, to recognize Your presence, and to follow Your direction. Let me be sensitive to Your leading, knowing that You are always speaking. Give me ears to listen and a heart that responds in obedience. Amen.

My Reflections & Prayer Notes:

_____
_____
_____
_____
_____
_____
_____
_____
_____
_____
_____
_____
_____
_____
_____
_____

Week 4: Walking It Out at Home

Scripture Focus:
"But as for me and my household, we will serve the Lord." (Joshua 24:15 NIV)

Weekly Focus:
Faith begins at home. This week, focus on how your faith impacts your family, marriage, and daily rhythms. Let your home be your first mission field and your heart a reflection of God's grace and strength.

Weekly Prayer:
Lord, help me to reflect Your love within my home. May my words, actions, and prayers create an atmosphere of faith, peace, and purpose. Let my home be a place where You dwell. Amen.

Day 22: The Great Commission Starts at Home

Scripture Focus: "Go therefore and make disciples of all nations, baptizing them in the name of the Father and of the Son and of the Holy Spirit, teaching them to observe all that I have commanded you. And behold, I am with you always, to the end of the age." (Matthew 28:19-20 NKJV)

Faith in Motion: Teaching Faith at Home

We often think of the Great Commission as a call for pastors, missionaries, or evangelists–those who travel far and wide to preach the Gospel. But discipleship begins right where we are. Our homes are our first mission field.

For years, I believed sharing the Gospel required a stage or a platform. I thought it meant leading Bible studies, speaking in front of crowds, or serving on mission trips. But God gently showed me that my greatest ministry started within the walls of my own home.

One of my most cherished memories is sitting at the foot of my daughter's bed in the evenings, Bible in hand, reading the Word of God aloud. I didn't understand everything I read, but I knew the Word was alive. I trusted that as I grew in Christ, He would help me understand—and He did.

To this day, my oldest daughter still remembers those quiet moments, listening to Scripture before falling asleep. Those bedtime Bible readings became seeds of faith planted in their hearts.

I learned that discipleship isn't always about perfect theology or eloquent prayers. It's about showing up, being present, and living a life that reflects Christ. It's in the way we speak to our children, how we respond to stress, and how we invite God's presence into our daily routines.

You don't have to be a Bible scholar to lead your family in faith—you just have to be willing to follow Jesus and bring your loved ones along with you.

Shaping Bodies & Hearts: Building a Foundation

In fitness, a strong foundation is essential. If we don't train properly from the beginning, our bodies will struggle with endurance and strength. Similarly, in faith, we must lay a foundation in our own homes before we can expect to impact the world.

Shaping Bodies: Foundation-Building Routine

This movement targets the core—your body's center of strength and stability—mirroring how a faith-filled home becomes the foundation for spiritual growth.

Exercise: Criss Cross (30–60 seconds):

- Lie on your back with your hands behind your head, knees bent, and feet lifted in tabletop position.
- Exhale as you lift your head, neck, and shoulders, twisting your torso to bring your right elbow toward your left knee while extending your right leg.
- Inhale as you return to center, then exhale and repeat on the other side.
- Continue alternating sides slowly and with control.

As you move, reflect on the strength it takes to build a Christ-centered home—where truth, love, and grace flow through every word and action.

Shaping Hearts: Making Disciples at Home

Model a Faith-Filled Life – Let those around you see your faith in action.

Pray Together as a Family – Establish regular times of prayer, no matter how short.

Share Scripture Daily – Whether reading aloud or writing a verse on a note, let God's Word be present in your home.

Encourage Faith Conversations – Ask questions, invite discussions, and create space for spiritual growth.

Dig Deeper

Invite Jesus into the rhythm of your household. Whether you share a verse, pray with a loved one, or simply respond with grace, let your home reflect the heart of the Great Commission.

Reflection & Prayer

Heavenly Father, thank You for calling me to make disciples, starting in my own home. Help me to live a life that reflects Your love, to be intentional in sharing Your truth, and to cultivate a home where faith flourishes. Give me wisdom and patience as I guide those closest to me. Amen.

My Reflections & Prayer Notes:

_____
_____
_____
_____
_____
_____
_____
_____
_____
_____

Day 23: Move Forward by Faith

Scripture Focus: "For we walk by faith, not by sight." (2 Corinthians 5:7 NKJV)

Faith in Motion: Pressing on Despite Fear

There are moments in life when we're faced with uncertainty or obstacles that make us want to stay put, afraid to take the next step. But God calls us to move forward by faith, even when we can't see the full picture. True faith isn't about having all the answers—it's about trusting that God is already ahead of us.

I remember a season when I felt completely stuck—unsure of my next step, doubting my ability to move forward in the calling I sensed God had placed on my heart. I kept waiting for a clear sign, hoping everything would line up before I acted. But the longer I waited, the more restless I became.

As I prayed, God reminded me: faith grows *in motion*. One of my favorite stories in Scripture—the woman with the issue of blood (Mark 5:25-34)—came to mind. After twelve years of suffering, she could have easily given up. But instead, she pushed through the crowd, past her fear, believing one touch from Jesus would change everything. And it did.

That story encouraged me to take a leap of faith when it came time to film my first *Shaped By Faith* TV pilot. I was searching for the perfect studio or filming location—overlooking the very space God had already prepared. He had given me my own home as the perfect setting to share faith and fitness with others. Filming that pilot in my home was both humbling and powerful. It was a reminder that when we step out in faith—even unsure or afraid—God meets us right where we are, often in the most unexpected ways.

Shaping Bodies & Hearts: Moving Forward to Gain Strength

In fitness, progress happens through movement. If we never challenge our bodies, we never grow stronger. The same is true spiritually—if we never step out in faith, we remain stagnant.

Shaping Bodies: Moving Forward in Strength

This workout reflects how faith requires movement—even when the path isn't clear. Forward and backward movements symbolize trusting God in both progress and setbacks, knowing He leads us every step.

Exercise: Forward Moving Knee Drives with Weights (15 seconds):

- Hold a set of light to moderate hand weights at shoulder height or down by your sides.
- Drive one knee up at a time while walking forward, engaging your core and lifting your chest high.
- Keep good posture and breathe steadily.

Imagine stepping into God's promises with each move.

Exercise: Backward Knee Drives (15 seconds):

- Continue holding the weights as you carefully step backward, alternating knees.
- Keep your core tight and eyes forward.

This challenges your balance and focus, reminding you that even when life seems to go in reverse, you're still in God's hands.

Repeat this forward and backward sequence 2–3 times.

To increase the challenge, raise the weights overhead as you move forward and bring them down toward your knee as you move backward.

As you move, declare, "I will press on. I will move forward. God is directing my steps."

Shaping Hearts: Trusting God's Path

Take One Bold Step – Identify an area where fear has held you back and commit to moving forward.

Replace Doubt with Truth – When uncertainty creeps in, declare God's promises over your situation.

Pray for Courage – Ask God for the strength to keep going, even when you can't see the outcome.

Celebrate Progress – Faith is a journey—recognize and thank God for each step along the way.

Dig Deeper

Faith moves. Identify one area where you've felt stuck and take a physical or spiritual step forward. It may be making a call, writing a prayer, or simply saying "yes" to God. If you'd like, record how it feels to move in His direction.

Reflection & Prayer

Heavenly Father, help me to move forward by faith, trusting that You are guiding my steps. Even when I don't see the full picture, I believe you are working for my good. Strengthen my heart, remove fear, and give me the courage to take the next step You are calling me to. Amen.

My Reflections & Prayer Notes:

Day 24: Tick-Tock, Tock-Tick

Scripture Focus: "About the ninth hour Jesus cried out in a loud voice, 'Eloi, Eloi, lama sabachthani?' which means, 'My God, my God, why have you forsaken me?" (Matthew 27:46 NKJV)

Faith in Motion: Time and Alignment

Our seventeen-month-old granddaughter, upon hearing "tick-tock, tick-tock," will immediately point to the nearest clock or watch. While her understanding of time is limited to things like bath time, lunch time, and potty time, she associates those words with time passing.

For many of us, our relationship with the clock can feel adversarial—we talk about "punching the clock" or trying to "beat the clock," yet no one can outrun time. We are all given a finite number of days, and while we can take care of our bodies through healthy eating, exercise, and rest, our time on earth is ultimately in God's hands.

"Then the Lord said, 'My Spirit will not contend with man forever, for he is mortal; his days will be a hundred and twenty years' (Genesis 6:3)."

Clockmakers describe timepieces that don't keep proper time as being "out of beat." Instead of tick-tock, they make a reversed sound—tock-tick. A clock that is out of beat needs adjustment to restore its alignment; otherwise, it serves no real purpose.

Spiritually, we too can become "out of beat" with God, misaligned by sin, distractions, and worldly priorities. But just as a skilled repairman can restore a broken clock, Jesus Christ came to set us back into alignment with the Father.

Shaping Bodies & Hearts: Staying in Rhythm

In fitness, rhythm and timing matter. Whether it's pacing in cardio exercises or executing movements with precision, being in sync with the right rhythm prevents injury and maximizes effectiveness. Similarly, our spiritual lives must stay aligned with God's timing rather than being rushed or delayed by personal desires.

Shaping Bodies: Rhythmic Strength Routine

This movement promotes balance, alignment, and strength—reminding us to stay in rhythm with God's purpose.

Exercise: Side Squats with Front Raise (30–60 seconds):

Stand tall with feet together and arms down by your sides (holding light weights if desired).

- Step your right foot out to the side and lower into a squat, keeping your chest lifted and knees behind your toes.
- At the same time, lift both arms straight in front of you to shoulder height.
- Push through your heels to return to standing, lowering your arms.
- Repeat on the left side and continue alternating.

Focus on smooth, controlled movement, exhaling as you lift and rising with strength and purpose.

As you move, ask God to align your body, mind, and spirit with His perfect rhythm.

Shaping Hearts: Aligning with God's Timing

Evaluate Your Priorities – Are your daily routines in sync with God's will, or do they need adjustment?

Trust in Divine Timing – Surrender control and trust that God's plans are unfolding at the right moment.

Stay Spiritually Tuned – Like maintaining a clock, regularly spending time in prayer and the Word to stay in alignment.

Be Watchful – Recognize when distractions or habits are pulling you away from God's rhythm and correct them quickly.

Dig Deeper

Ask God to show you where your life may be out of beat. Is there a place where you're rushing ahead or falling behind His timing? Invite Him to reset your spiritual rhythm so you can walk in step with His purpose.

Reflection & Prayer

Heavenly Father, help me to stay in rhythm with Your perfect timing. When I rush ahead or lag behind, remind me to trust in Your divine plan. Align my heart, mind, and body with Your will so that I may walk in step with You every day. Amen.

My Reflections & Prayer Notes:

_____

_____

_____

_____

_____

_____

Day 25: Pressing On with Endurance

Scripture Focus: "Let us run with endurance the race that is set before us, looking to Jesus, the founder and perfecter of our faith." (Hebrews 12:1-2 NKJV)

Faith in Motion: Running the Race of Faith

The Christian life is often described as a race—not a sprint, but a marathon of faith. There are seasons where we feel strong, running with joy and purpose. There are also moments of exhaustion, setbacks, and trials that tempt us to stop. The key is to keep our eyes on Jesus and press on with endurance.

I remember participating in a race where I started strong, full of energy and excitement. But halfway through, my legs grew tired, my breath became heavy, and I was tempted to slow down. Just as I considered stopping, I saw a familiar face cheering me on from the sidelines, encouraging me to keep going. That moment gave me the boost I needed to push through the fatigue and finish the race.

This reminded me of how God places encouragement and strength along our faith journey. When we feel weak, He provides the motivation we need—through scripture, through others, and through His Spirit within us. Endurance isn't about never feeling tired; it's about choosing to keep going despite the struggle.

Shaping Bodies & Hearts: Training for Endurance

Building endurance in fitness requires persistence and consistent effort. If we quit when we get tired, we never increase our stamina. The same is true in faith—we grow stronger by pressing on, even when we feel like giving up.

Shaping Bodies: Endurance Training Routine

This workout focuses on building stamina and resilience, mirroring the steady perseverance we need on our faith journey.

Exercise: Step-Ups with Biceps Curl (30-60 seconds):

- Step onto a sturdy bench or platform with your right foot, curling the weights as you rise.
- Step down and repeat on the other side.

This movement builds leg strength and upper body endurance—just like taking steady steps of faith.

Exercise: Alternating Reverse Lunges with Lateral Raise (30-60 seconds):

- Step back into a lunge with one leg while raising your arms out to the sides.
- Return to standing and switch legs.

This full-body movement strengthens both your balance and resolve.

As you move, focus on the truth that endurance is not built in a moment—but through persistence, prayer, and trusting God with each step forward.

Shaping Hearts: Pressing On in Faith

Fix Your Eyes on Jesus -- When distractions or discouragement come, refocus on Him.

Find Encouragement – Surround yourself with others who inspire you to keep going.

Take One Step at a Time -- Don't be overwhelmed by the whole race—just focus on the next step.

Rest When Needed – Even endurance runners take moments to refuel and recover—allow God to refresh you in His presence. Rest for at least one day or consider resting for two days. I always rest on the weekends, taking two days off to recover and reset.

Dig Deeper

Picture your faith journey as a long, steady race. You may not see the finish line, but Jesus is alongside you, cheering you on. Take a moment to thank Him for His strength, and keep moving forward—one step, one breath, one prayer at a time.

Reflection & Prayer

Heavenly Father, give me the strength to run this race with endurance. When I feel weary, remind me that You are my source of energy and perseverance. Help me to press on, trusting that You have prepared the path ahead of me. Amen.

My Reflections & Prayer Notes:

_____
_____
_____
_____
_____
_____
_____
_____
_____

Day 26: God Makes All Things New

Scripture Focus: "Therefore, if anyone is in Christ, the new creation has come: The old has gone, the new is here!" (2 Corinthians 5:17 NIV)

Faith in Motion: Embracing New Beginnings

God is in the business of restoration and renewal. No matter what we have been through—our past mistakes, failures, or struggles—He offers us a fresh start. When we surrender to Him, He doesn't just improve us; He makes us new.

There was a time in my life when I felt defined by my past. I had made mistakes, faced disappointments, and wondered if I had drifted too far for God to restore me. But then, God reminded me of His promise: He makes all things new.

One moment in particular stands out. I had been carrying the weight of past failures, replaying them in my mind, feeling unworthy of a fresh start. But as I prayed, I felt God speak to my heart: "Let it go. I have already made you new." That truth changed everything. Instead of living in regret, I began walking in the newness of His grace, trusting that He had a greater plan going forward.

Shaping Bodies & Hearts: Renewal Through Movement

In fitness, we experience renewal every time we strengthen our bodies. When we train, our muscles tear slightly, and as they repair, they become stronger. Similarly, when we allow God to work in us, He takes what was broken and makes it whole, renewing our spirit and faith.

Shaping Bodies: Renewal & Restoration Routine

This workout focuses on rebuilding strength and embracing renewal—physically and spiritually.

Exercise: Bridge with Skull Crushers (30-60 seconds):

- Lie on your back with knees bent and feet flat on the floor.
- Hold weights and extend your arms straight above your chest.
- As you lift your hips into a bridge, lower the weights by bending your elbows (skull crusher).
- Press the weights back up as you lower your hips.

This compound move renews both upper body and core strength.

Exercise: High Bridge Hold with Chest Fly (30-60 seconds):

- Hold the bridge position with hips lifted.
- With weights in hand, extend arms above chest and slowly open them out to the sides in a chest fly, then return to center.
- Maintain the bridge to engage glutes and hamstrings, while the fly opens your heart and posture.

As you move, focus on letting go of the past and embracing the newness God offers. Allow each breath and movement to be an act of surrender and trust in His power to restore.

Shaping Hearts: Walking in Newness

Release the Past – Identify areas where you are holding onto old regrets and give them to God.

Embrace God's Renewal – Declare daily that you are a new creation in Christ.

Step Forward in Faith – Leave behind what no longer serves you and trust God's new plan for your life.

Praise God for Your Transformation – Thank Him for His work in your life, even when you can't see the full picture yet.

Dig Deeper

Is there something weighing on your spirit or lingering in your thoughts that needs God's renewing touch? Ask Him to make it new. If you feel led, write down one way He's restoring your spirit, renewing your mind, or strengthening your body right now.

Reflection & Prayer

Heavenly Father, thank You for making me new. I release my past into Your hands and embrace the renewal You offer. Help me to walk forward in faith, trusting that You are restoring me daily. May my heart, mind, and body reflect the transformation You are doing within me. Amen.

My Reflections & Prayer Notes:

_____
_____
_____
_____
_____
_____
_____
_____
_____

Day 27: Living Victoriously in Christ

Scripture Focus: "But thanks be to God! He gives us the victory through our Lord Jesus Christ." (1 Corinthians 15:57 NIV)

As followers of Christ, we are not called to live in defeat but to walk in victory. The battles we face, whether physical, emotional, or spiritual, do not define us. Instead, Christ's finished work on the cross has already secured our victory. When we stand on His promises, we can move forward with confidence, knowing that we are more than conquerors.

Faith in Motion: Finding Victory in Christ

There was a time in my life when I felt overwhelmed by challenges. No matter how hard I tried, I felt like I was always fighting an uphill battle. I prayed for breakthroughs, but the obstacles remained. I began to wonder if I would ever experience the victory that scripture spoke of. I felt trapped in a cycle of struggle and striving, desperately wanting to move forward but unsure how.

One season stands out in my memory. I had reached a point where I was physically exhausted, emotionally drained, and spiritually weary. I had done everything I knew to do—prayed, sought advice, and worked tirelessly to overcome the situation—but nothing seemed to change. One day, in sheer frustration, I cried out to God, "Lord, I can't do this anymore! I need You to fight this battle for me!"

In that moment, a peace settled over me. I realized that victory wasn't about my strength—it was about surrendering to God's power. I had been relying on my own efforts instead of fully trusting Him. From that day forward, I began declaring God's truth over my life. I stood on His promises, knowing that He had already won the battle for me. I stopped letting fear control me and stepped forward in faith, walking in the victory that was already mine in Christ.

That shift in mindset changed everything. No matter what came my way, I faced it with the confidence of someone who knew they had already won. It didn't mean life suddenly became easy, but it did mean I had a new perspective—one of faith, not fear. God had equipped me for victory, and all I needed to do was trust Him to lead me through.

Instead of striving in my own effort, I began declaring God's truth over my life. I stood on His promises, knowing that He had already won the battle for me. I stopped letting fear control me and stepped forward in faith, walking in the victory that was already mine in Christ. That shift in mindset changed everything. No matter what came my way, I faced it with the confidence of someone who knew they had already won.

Shaping Bodies & Hearts: Training with a Victor's Mindset

In fitness, our mindset determines our success. If we believe we are too weak or incapable, we are more likely to quit. But when we train with the mindset of a champion, we push past obstacles, knowing that every challenge makes us stronger. Likewise, in faith, when we stand in Christ's victory, we face trials with boldness, knowing that He has already overcome.

Shaping Bodies: Victory Strength Routine

This workout builds confidence and strength, reinforcing a mindset of victory.

Exercise: Weighted Elbow to Knee Crunch (30–60 seconds):

- Stand tall, holding a light to moderate weight at your chest.
- Lift your right knee as you twist your torso, bringing your left elbow toward the knee.
- Return to start and alternate sides.

This move engages your core and symbolizes crushing lies and obstacles with God's truth.

Exercise: Weighted T-Stance (30-60 seconds):

- Hold a light weight in each hand.
- Shift your weight onto one leg, hinging forward slightly as the opposite leg lifts behind you, forming a T shape with your body.
- Extend arms out to the sides, maintaining balance and core engagement.
- Switch legs after 30 seconds.

This exercise strengthens balance and posture, reminding you to remain steady and victorious in Christ.

As you move, declare victory over any challenge you are facing in Jesus' name—He has already won the battle on your behalf.

Shaping Hearts: Walking in Victory Daily

Speak Truth Over Your Life – Replace fear with scripture-based declarations of victory.

Pray with Boldness – Approach God knowing that He has already secured your victory.

Celebrate Small Wins – Recognize moments of growth and acknowledge God's work in your life.

Encourage Others – Share your testimony of victory to inspire those around you.

Dig Deeper

Ask the Lord to reveal where your spirit has been discouraged, where your mind has rehearsed defeat, or where your body has felt weak. Invite Him to restore you in each area. If you'd like, write down a scripture that reminds you to live in victory.

Reflection & Prayer

Heavenly Father, thank You for the victory I have in Christ. When I feel weak, remind me that You have already overcome. Help me to stand in faith, move forward with confidence, and live boldly as a child of victory. Let my life reflect the power of Your resurrection. Amen.

My Reflections & Prayer Notes:

_____
_____
_____
_____
_____
_____
_____
_____
_____
_____

Day 28: Finishing Strong

Scripture Focus: "I have fought the good fight, I have finished the race, I have kept the faith." (2 Timothy 4:7 NIV)

The journey of faith and fitness is not about perfection; it's about perseverance. God doesn't call us to start strong only to quit when things get difficult. Instead, He calls us to run with endurance, to press on even when we feel weary, and to finish strong in Him.

Faith in Motion: Pushing Through to the Finish

I will never forget one of the toughest races I ever ran. I had trained for it, prepared mentally and physically, but halfway through, exhaustion hit me like a wall. Every part of me wanted to stop. My legs felt like lead, my breathing was heavy, and my mind began to question whether I could do it.

But then, I remembered why I started. I thought about the training, the preparation, and the goal that was just ahead. I whispered a prayer, asking God for strength, and I kept moving forward—one step at a time. When I finally reached the finish line, the feeling was indescribable. Not just because I had completed the race, but because I had pushed through when I wanted to quit.

Faith is the same way. There are seasons when we feel exhausted, discouraged, or uncertain. But God doesn't ask us to run in our strength—He provides what we need to endure and finish strong. When we rely on Him, He empowers us to cross the finish line victoriously.

Shaping Bodies & Hearts: The Power of Endurance

In fitness, finishing a workout requires mental and physical endurance. It's not always about speed; it's about consistency and determination. The same is true in our spiritual walk—when we fix our eyes on Christ, He gives us the strength to persevere.

Shaping Bodies: Finishing Strong Routine

This workout encourages persistence and endurance—physically and spiritually.

Exercise: Alternate Lateral Lunge & Press (30-60 seconds):

- Step out to the side into a lateral lunge while holding weights at shoulder height.
- As you return to center, press the weights overhead.
- Alternate sides.

This movement builds lower-body strength and reminds us to press on in faith.

Exercise: Alternate Reverse Lunge & Hammer Curl (30–60 seconds):

- Step back into a reverse lunge while performing a hammer curl with your weights.
- Return to standing and switch legs.

This combination strengthens your foundation and upper body, reinforcing perseverance and control.

As you move, declare: "I will finish strong in faith, with the strength and grace God provides!"

Shaping Hearts: Strength to Finish Well

Stay Consistent in Prayer – Keep communication with God daily, even in difficult seasons.

Hold Tight to God's Promises – Meditate on scriptures that remind you of His faithfulness.

Encourage Others to Keep Going – Be a source of support and motivation for those running their race.

Celebrate Progress, Not Perfection – Acknowledge how far you've come and trust God for what's ahead.

Dig Deeper

Ask God to renew your spirit with strength to endure. Shift your mindset from weariness to hope by declaring His promises. Then move your body with determination, letting every step remind you that you are finishing strong in His grace.

Reflection & Prayer

Heavenly Father, thank You for giving me the strength to endure. Help me to keep my eyes on You and to finish strong, trusting that You are leading me every step of the way. No matter the challenges, I know you provide the endurance I need. I commit to pressing on in faith until I cross the finish line in victory. Amen.

My Reflections & Prayer Notes:

_____
_____
_____
_____
_____
_____
_____
_____

Week 5: Staying the Course

Scripture Focus:
"Let us run with endurance the race God has set before us. We do this by keeping our eyes on Jesus." (Hebrews 12:1-2)

Weekly Focus:
This week may test your consistency but stay the course. Remember, God is faithful to finish what He starts. Even when you're tired or tempted to give up, keep your eyes fixed on Jesus and take the next step.

Weekly Prayer:
Father, help me to persevere when the path feels long. Strengthen my resolve and help me stay focused on You. Thank You for being my steady guide and my strength. Amen.

Day 29: Honoring God with Every Rep

Scripture Focus: "Be strong in the Lord and in His mighty power." (Ephesians 6:10)

Faith in Motion: Strength in Weakness

After my second open-heart surgery to repair three holes in my heart, I was told to wait six weeks before returning to physical activity. But at just four weeks post-op, I felt an urgency—one not from pride, but from divine purpose. No cardiac rehab was recommended, so I created my own: strength training.

Each rep hurt—especially the overhead presses that stretched my healing sternum—but I prayed through it. I returned to teaching fitness classes, and my students cheered me on as I asked the Lord to give me the strength and endurance to run this race with excellence. And He did.

I learned firsthand that when we offer even our weakest moments to God, He meets us with His power. Every breath, every movement became an act of worship. I wasn't just exercising, I was honoring God with the body He entrusted to me.

Shaping Bodies & Hearts: Worship in Motion

Strength training, like spiritual growth, is about more than physical effort. It's about honoring God in the process. When we approach exercise with a heart of gratitude and worship, it becomes a sacred act, a living sacrifice offered back to Him.

As Romans 12:1 reminds us, our true worship is offering our bodies as living sacrifices. Each rep can renew the mind (Romans 12:2), develop perseverance (Romans 5:3–4), and cultivate joy (Proverbs 17:22). In fitness and faith alike, strength is built not just in power—but in purpose.

Shaping Bodies: Worshipful Strength Circuit

Do this circuit 2–3 times, focusing on form and worshipful intention.

1. **Overhead Press (15 reps):** Visualize pressing your praises upward as you build strength.
   - Stand with feet shoulder-width apart, holding dumbbells at shoulder height, palms facing forward.
   - Engage your core and press the weights straight overhead until arms are fully extended but avoid locking elbows.
   - Lower slowly back to shoulder height.
   - Keep your movements controlled, breathing out as you press up and in as you lower.

2. **Plank Hold (30–60 seconds):** Ground yourself in God's power.
   - Begin on the floor, resting on your forearms with elbows directly under your shoulders.
   - Extend your legs behind you, balancing on your toes so your body forms a straight line from head to heels.
   - Engage your core, glutes, and legs, keeping your hips level.
   - Keep your neck neutral, eyes down, and focus on steady breathing as you hold.

3. **Bodyweight Squats (15 reps):** Root yourself in gratitude with each controlled movement.
   - Stand with feet hip- to shoulder-width apart, toes slightly turned out.
   - Keeping chest lifted and core engaged, push hips back as if sitting into a chair.
   - Lower until thighs are parallel to the ground (or as low as comfortable), keeping knees in line with toes.
   - Press through heels to return to standing, squeezing glutes at the top.
   - Move at a steady pace, breathing out as you rise and in as you lower.

Each movement becomes a declaration: "Lord, I honor You with my body."

Shaping Hearts: Daily Strength Check-In

Reflect – Where do you need God's strength today—physically, emotionally, spiritually?

Reframe Your Mindset – Choose to see your movement as worship, not obligation.

Declare This Truth -- "I am strong in the Lord and in His mighty power." (Ephesians 6:10)

Encourage Someone – Text or call a friend with a word of strength and scripture.

Dig Deeper:

Ask God for strength in your spirit today. Renew your mind by declaring, "I AM STRONG IN THE LORD AND IN HIS MIGHTY POWER." Then move your body as worship—choose one workout this week to dedicate fully to Him, and let every rep be an offering of praise.

Reflection & Prayer

Lord, thank You for the strength You provide—especially when I feel weak. Help me see every movement, breath, and workout as an offering of worship to You. Remind me that my body is Your temple and that through You, I have strength for today. May I honor You in every rep, every step, and every act of obedience. In Jesus' name, amen.

My Reflections & Prayer Notes:

Day 30: The Heart of God

Scripture Focus: "The Lord is gracious and compassionate, slow to anger and rich in love." (Psalm 145:8 NIV)

Faith in Motion: Understanding God's Love

We live in a world where love is often conditional based on performance, approval, or what we can offer. But God's heart is completely different. His love is unfailing, unchanging, and unlimited. No matter what we do or where we go, His heart is always for us.

I remember a time when I struggled to understand God's love for me. I had grown up knowing about His love, but truly believing that His heart was turned toward me—even when I made mistakes—was a different story. I often felt like I had to work harder, do more, and prove myself worthy of His affection.

Then one day, as I sat in quiet prayer, I felt His presence overwhelm me. It wasn't in a booming voice or dramatic sign—it was in the stillness, the deep assurance that I was fully known and fully loved. I realized that God's heart wasn't based on my performance but on who He is. He is gracious, compassionate, and rich in love—always waiting for His children to turn to Him.

Shaping Bodies & Hearts: The Heart of It All

Just as our physical heart sustains our body, our spiritual heart is the center of our faith life. In fitness, we train our cardiovascular system to increase strength and endurance. Spiritually, we build heart strength by drawing near to God, trusting in His love, and walking in His compassion.

Shaping Bodies: Heart-Strengthening Routine

This workout builds endurance and resilience—mirroring our growing relationship with God.

Exercise: Side-to-Side Steps with Prayer Focus (30–60 seconds): Move rhythmically while meditating on God's love.

Exercise: Stability Ball Crunch (30–60 seconds): Engage your core and reflect on the steadfast nature of God's heart for you.

Exercise: Step Repeaters (30–60 seconds): Keep your heart strong and focused on His unwavering love.

As you move, remind yourself: *God's heart is always for me.*

Spiritual Exercise: Shaping Hearts – Drawing Closer to God's Heart

- Sit quietly in God's presence and simply receive His love.
- Read and reflect on scriptures that describe His compassion and faithfulness.
- Ask God to shape your heart to mirror His.
- Show grace and kindness to someone in your life who needs to experience the love of Christ.

Dig Deeper

Rest in God's love today—He sees you, knows you, and delights in you. Let His truth renew your mind as you reflect on **Psalm 145:8**. Then move your body with gratitude, letting each step remind you: GOD'S HEART IS ALWAYS FOR ME.

Reflection & Prayer

Heavenly Father, thank You for Your gracious and compassionate heart. Help me to rest in Your love, knowing I don't have to earn it—I only need to receive it. Shape my heart to reflect Yours and guide me in loving others with the same grace You've shown me. Amen.

My Reflections & Prayer Notes:

Day 31: The Joy of the Lord is My Strength

Scripture Focus: "The joy of the Lord is your strength." (Nehemiah 8:10)

Faith in Motion: Strength That Smiles Back at Life

Joy is not just a pleasant feeling—it's spiritual power. In Nehemiah 8, God's people were weeping over their failures, but the Lord told them not to grieve, because His joy would strengthen them for the days ahead. Joy does not ignore the reality of hardships, but it refuses to let hardships have the final word.

I've learned that joy is like a hidden well. Sometimes I reach for it when I feel strong and full of gratitude. Other times, I have to draw deeply when I feel weary, burdened, or worn thin. Joy is not something I have to manufacture—it flows from knowing who God is and remembering that He is faithful, even when my circumstances aren't what I hoped for.

One season in my life, I found myself smiling through tears. The challenges hadn't disappeared, but my focus shifted.

Instead of constantly replaying my problems in my mind, I started rehearsing God's goodness. I sang worship songs while doing chores. I thanked Him for small blessings. I laughed more, even when I didn't feel like it. Slowly, my heart felt lighter, my steps steadier. It was then I understood—His joy wasn't just making me *happy*, it was making me *strong*.

Shaping Bodies & Hearts: Training with Joy

In fitness, attitude can fuel endurance. A workout approached with dread feels longer and heavier, but when we add joy—thanking God for a body that moves, celebrating progress—it changes the entire experience. The same is true in our spiritual walk. Joy lifts the weight off our souls and keeps us moving forward when fatigue sets in.

Shaping Bodies: Joyful Strength Routine

This workout builds confidence and strength, reinforcing a mindset of victory and joy.

Exercise: Kettlebell Swing with a Smile (30-60 seconds): As you swing the weight, focus on good form—and intentionally smile. This simple act signals your body to release feel-good endorphins.

Exercise: Praise Squats (30-60 seconds): With or without weights, squat down while lifting your hands in praise as you rise. Imagine handing your burdens to the Lord as you lift.

Exercise: Lateral Step with Thanksgiving (30-60 seconds): Step side to side with resistance band or body weight, naming one blessing with each step.

Shaping Hearts: Choosing Joy Daily

- Start the day with gratitude for three things.
- Meditate on a joyful Scripture like Psalm 16:11.
- Share a laugh or encouragement with someone.
- Worship, even if your heart feels heavy.

Dig Deeper

Ask yourself: Where have I been letting discouragement steal my joy? What's one thing I can do today to intentionally stir up the joy of the Lord?

Reflection & Prayer

Heavenly Father, thank You for the joy that strengthens me from the inside out. Help me to choose joy when I feel weak and to draw from Your well of gladness when my heart feels dry. Let my life be marked by a joy that reflects Your presence and points others to You. Amen.

My Reflections & Prayer Notes:

Day 32: Living for Jesus – The Next Generation

Scripture Focus: "We will not hide them from their descendants; we will tell the next generation the praiseworthy deeds of the LORD, his power, and the wonders he has done." (Psalm 78:4)

Faith in Motion: Called to Be Good Stewards

God calls us to be faithful stewards of His Word and to share His mighty works with those who come after us. The testimonies of our faith journeys encourage the next generation to trust God and walk boldly in their calling.

One of the greatest joys in my life has been watching young people grow in their faith and step into their God-given purpose. I think back to the many times I have led fitness classes, Bible studies, and women's conferences, seeing the light of Christ shine in the next generation. Their passion, hunger for truth, and desire to make a difference inspire me daily.

I remember a young woman who came to one of my fitness and faith sessions. She had struggled with self-worth, battling the pressures of social media and cultural expectations. Through our workouts and devotionals, she began to see herself through God's eyes. She realized that her worth was not found in her appearance or achievements but in being a beloved daughter of the King. Now, she leads a Bible study for young women, teaching them to stand firm in their identity in Christ.

Shaping Bodies & Hearts: Training Up The Next Generation

Just as we pass down wisdom and encouragement to the next generation spiritually, we do the same physically. Training young people in good health habits equips them to serve God with strength and endurance. Paul instructs us in **1 Timothy 4:8**, "For physical training is of some value, but godliness has value for all things, holding promise for both the present life and the life to come."

Teaching proper form in exercise ensures injury prevention and long-term success. Similarly, guiding the next generation in their faith walk provides them with a solid foundation to withstand life's challenges. When we model a lifestyle of prayer, worship, and scripture study, we show them how to maintain spiritual endurance.

Shaping Bodies: Core Strength Training

Building a strong core is essential for stability and endurance in fitness. A strong core supports every movement—from walking and lifting to maintaining posture. Just as a firm foundation in faith keeps us steady, a strong core helps us move with confidence and purpose.

Exercise: Core Stability Routine:

- **Forearm Plank Hold (30–60 seconds):** Lower onto your forearms, keeping elbows beneath your shoulders. Engage your core, glutes, and legs while holding your body in a straight line. Focus on spiritual stillness and strength in the waiting.
- **High Plank Mountain Climbers (30–60 seconds):** From a high plank position, alternate driving your knees toward your chest. Keep your core tight and move with rhythm, visualizing yourself running the race of faith with endurance.

As you strengthen your physical core, reflect on how your spiritual core—rooted in Christ—keeps you grounded through life's challenges.

Shaping Hearts: Discipleship and Mentorship

As we build physical strength, let's also commit to strengthening the next generation in faith. Identify a young person in your life whom you can encourage and mentor. Share your faith story, offer guidance, and be a source of wisdom. If you don't have someone in mind, pray for God to place someone in your path.

Encourage Someone – Write a letter or send a message of encouragement to a young believer.

Invite Someone to Bible Study – Invite them to join you in a Bible study or devotional time.

Be Mindful of Your Behavior – Model a Christ-centered lifestyle through your words and actions.

Get a Workout Buddy – Invite a younger person to join you in a faith-based exercise class.

Dig Deeper

Ask God to show you one young person to invest in this week. Whether through a simple word of encouragement, sharing your story, or inviting them to grow in faith, be intentional in passing on strength and truth to the next generation.

Reflection and Prayer

Heavenly Father, thank You for the opportunity to impact the next generation. Help me be a godly example, sharing Your truth and love with those who come after me. Give me wisdom to mentor and disciple, and may my life reflect Your goodness and faithfulness. Strengthen me physically and spiritually to serve You wholeheartedly. In Jesus' name, amen.

My Reflections & Prayer Notes:

Day 33: There is Purpose in Our Pain

Scripture Focus: "What we suffer now is nothing compared to the glory he will reveal to us later." (Romans 8:18)

Faith in Motion: Purpose in the Pain

At one time or another, most of us have experienced pain beyond our limits—an eleven on a scale of ten. Whether emotional heartache, physical suffering, or a broken spirit piercing our soul, we all go through painful seasons. It is natural to wonder why we endure these struggles and if they will ever end.

When the Apostle Paul faced a thorn in his flesh, he pleaded with God to remove it. Yet, God denied his request, instead assuring him: "My grace is sufficient for you, for my power is made perfect in weakness." (2 Corinthians 12:9). Paul's suffering had a purpose—to keep him humble and reliant on God's strength.

Reflecting on my own experiences, I recently had a knee procedure to help with chronic pain. I wasn't expecting more pain in the process! But healing often comes through discomfort. Just as Paul found purpose in his suffering, I realized that my pain was teaching me patience, endurance, and total dependence on God.

Shaping Bodies & Hearts: Pain is Transformative

Pain is often necessary for growth, both physically and spiritually. In fitness, muscle soreness is a sign of progress. When we push our bodies beyond their comfort zones, micro-tears in the muscle fibers must heal, making us stronger. The same principle applies to our faith—God refines us through trials to develop perseverance and deepen our trust in Him.

Rather than resisting discomfort, we can embrace it as part of God's greater plan for transformation. "For our present troubles are small and won't last very long. Yet they produce for us a glory that vastly outweighs them and will last forever!" (2 Corinthians 4:17).

Shaping Bodies: Strength Through Resistance Training

Pain is part of the process when building strength. Resistance training teaches us to push through discomfort, just as we push through life's challenges with faith and perseverance.

Exercise: Strength Routine:

- **Bodyweight Squats (15 reps):** Stand with feet hip-width apart, lower into a squat as if sitting back in a chair, then rise back up with control.
- **Wall Sit (Hold for 30 seconds to 1 minute):** Stand against a wall and slide down until your knees are at a 90-degree angle. Hold the position, engaging your core and legs.
- **Reverse Lunges (15 reps per leg):** Step one foot back and lower into a lunge, keeping your front knee aligned over your ankle. Return to standing and switch legs.

Repeat the circuit 2-3 times, focusing on controlled movements, steady breathing, and trusting that each step of resistance builds greater endurance—physically and spiritually.

Shaping Hearts: Finding Purpose in Pain

Journal – Write down a past or present pain that has strengthened your faith.

Meditate – Read **Romans 8:18** and ask God to reveal His purpose in your suffering.

Be Grateful – Instead of complaining about discomfort, thank God for His refining work in you.

Encourage Others – Offer encouragement to someone who is going through a painful season.

Dig Deeper

When you face pain this week—physical or emotional—pause and pray. Ask God to reveal His purpose in it and to strengthen your faith through the process. Let every moment of discomfort become an opportunity to grow in trust and endurance.

Reflection and Prayer

Heavenly Father, help me to see my pain through Your eyes. Remind me that You are working all things for my good, even when I don't understand. Strengthen my faith and endurance as I walk through trials. May my struggles glorify You and encourage others. In Jesus' name, amen.

My Reflections & Prayer Notes:

_____
_____
_____
_____
_____
_____
_____
_____
_____

Day 34: Do Not Quit

Scripture Focus: "So, dear brothers, work hard to prove that you really are among those God has called and chosen. Do these things, and you will never fall away. Then God will give you a grand entrance into the eternal Kingdom of our Lord and Savior Jesus Christ." (2 Peter 1:10-11)

Faith in Motion: Forgiveness is Key

If we are honest with ourselves, most of us have said or done things we wish we could take back. Sometimes, we speak before understanding the full story, leading to misunderstandings. I had such a moment during one of my son's cross-country races.

As I stood in the spectator area, I saw him slowing down midway through the race. Concerned that he was giving up, I yelled words of encouragement, urging him to push harder. Little did I know he was battling intense pain. His focus remained ahead, determined to finish the race. When he crossed the finish line, his body collapsed, and he clutched his foot in agony. I assumed he was being dramatic until he told me, "I think my foot is broken." Sure enough, an x-ray later confirmed it.

I felt awful, realizing that my words during the race had been spoken in ignorance. His coach, too, had misjudged the situation. But in that moment, I saw an important lesson—perseverance isn't just about enduring physically but also having the heart to push forward despite pain and doubt. My son finished the race injured, yet with determination. Not only did he complete the race, but he also scored for his team that day, demonstrating true perseverance and commitment. His ability to forgive his coach and me required a strength that came from his faith in God.

Shaping Bodies & Hearts: Perseverance

Perseverance is a fundamental principle in both faith and fitness. Just as an athlete must train consistently and push through discomfort to build endurance, we must develop spiritual endurance. In moments of hardship, giving up may seem like the easiest option, but God calls us to persevere.

The Apostle Peter encouraged believers to build their faith like strengthening muscles—layer by layer, adding moral excellence, knowledge, self-control, and endurance (2 Peter 1:5-9). Similarly, in fitness, consistent training builds endurance, allowing us to go farther and stronger than before. When we refuse to quit, we build not only physical stamina but also a resilient faith that stands the test of time.

Shaping Bodies: Endurance Training

Perseverance in fitness requires building stamina. This workout focuses on endurance and mental toughness—training your body to keep going even when it gets challenging, just like we press forward in faith during trials.

Exercise: Endurance Routine:

- **Step Ups (1 minute):** Using a sturdy bench or step, step up with one foot, then the other. Step back down and repeat, alternating lead legs. For added challenge, hold weights in each hand.
- **Weighted Squats (15 reps):** Stand with feet hip-width apart, holding a weight in each hand. Lower into a squat, keeping your chest lifted and knees behind your toes. Rise with control.
- **Weighted Reverse Lunges (15 reps per leg):** Holding weights, step one foot back into a lunge, keeping your front knee aligned over your ankle. Return to standing and switch legs.

Repeat the circuit 2-3 times, focusing on steady breathing, controlled movement, and unwavering perseverance—both physically and spiritually.

Shaping Hearts: Strengthening Your Faith Endurance

Reflect -- Think on a time when you wanted to give up. How did God give you the strength to keep going?

Meditate -- Read **2 Peter 1:10-11**, asking God to build endurance in your faith.

Journal – Write down an area in your life where you feel tempted to quit.

Pray – Ask God for perseverance and seek His guidance.

Encourage – Think of someone who is struggling, remind them of God's promises.

Dig Deeper

This week, when you feel tempted to quit—whether in fitness, faith, or life—pause and pray. Ask God for the strength to keep going. Trust that every step forward in perseverance draws you closer to the victory He has prepared.

Reflection and Prayer

Heavenly Father, thank You for calling me to a life of perseverance. Help me to push forward in faith, even when I feel weak or discouraged. Strengthen my endurance, both spiritually and physically, so that I may run the race You have set before me. May my determination glorify You and inspire others to keep going. In Jesus' name, amen.

My Reflections & Prayer Notes:

Day 35: Matters of the Heart – Aligning Our Emotions with God's Will

Scripture Focus: "Come close to God, and God will come close to you." (James 4:8)

Faith in Motion: Guard Your Heart

Our hearts are the center of our emotions, desires, and decisions. The Bible tells us that God is deeply concerned with the state of our hearts because it influences everything we do. "Above all else, guard your heart, for everything you do flows from it (Proverbs 4:23)."

On our farm, we have an electric fence to keep the cattle within their boundaries, but perhaps more importantly, it prevents them from wandering into dangerous areas. In the same way, God reminds us to guard our hearts before our emotions shape our actions and relationships. When we surrender our hearts to Christ, we experience true peace and fulfillment.

One of the most powerful examples of a heart aligned with God is David. Despite his failures, he consistently sought the Lord, repenting when he fell short. "I have found David, son of Jesse, a man after my own heart. He will do everything I want him to do (Acts 13:22)." David's prayers in Psalms reflect a deep and desperate longing for God: "Create in me a pure heart, O God, and renew a steadfast spirit within me (Psalm 51:10)."

When I feel overwhelmed by emotions, Psalm 42:11 reminds me to shift my focus from feelings to faith: "Why am I discouraged? Why is my heart so sad? I will put my hope in God! I will praise him again—my Savior and my God!"

Shaping Bodies & Hearts: Discipline and Consistency

Just as we need to guard our hearts spiritually, we must also strengthen them physically. The heart is a muscle that requires both protection and training to function properly. Cardiovascular exercise helps our hearts grow stronger, allowing us to endure challenges with greater resilience. Similarly, a heart rooted in Christ builds endurance to withstand emotional and spiritual battles.

When we neglect heart health—whether physically or spiritually—we open the door to weakness. But when we exercise discipline, staying consistent in both fitness and faith, we experience lasting strength.

Shaping Bodies: Heart-Strengthening Cardio Workout

Just as we are called to guard our spiritual hearts, we must also care for our physical hearts with intentional movement that builds endurance and resilience.

Exercise: Heart-Strengthening Cardio Routine:

- **Fast Walking (5 to 10 minutes):** Warm up your body and increase your heart rate with a steady, purposeful pace.
- **Step Ups (1 to 2 minutes):** Use a sturdy platform or step. Alternate legs as you step up and down to elevate your heart rate and build lower-body strength.
- **Kettlebell Swings (1 to 2 minutes):** Swing the kettlebell with control, engaging your core and glutes. (Use a single weight if a kettlebell is not available.)
- **Plank with Mountain Climbers (1 minute):** In a high plank, drive knees toward your chest one at a time, keeping your body strong and stable.

Repeat the circuit 2-3 times, focusing on your breath and the steady strength God gives you with every heartbeat.

Shaping Hearts: Aligning Your Heart with God's Will

Reflect on **Proverbs 4:23** – How well are you guarding your heart?

Journal – Write about any emotions or desires that may be leading you away from God's best.

Pray – Ask God to align your heart with His will, surrendering any emotional burdens.

Share God's Love - Identify one relationship where you need to apply **1 Corinthians 13:4**'s definition of love.

Dig Deeper

This week, strengthen your heart—both physically and spiritually. Commit to at least three cardio workouts and take time in prayer to reflect on any emotions or desires that need to be realigned with God's will. Ask Him to guard and guide your heart in all things.

Reflection and Prayer

Heavenly Father, I surrender my heart to You. Align my desires with Your will, heal any brokenness, and help me love others as You love me. Thank You for Your grace that strengthens both my heart and my faith. In Jesus' name, amen.

My Reflections & Prayer Notes:

My Reflections & Prayer Notes

Week 6: Finishing Strong

Scripture Focus:
"I have fought the good fight, I have finished the race, and I have remained faithful." (2 Timothy 4:7)

Weekly Focus:
You've made it to the final stretch! This week is about finishing with faith, gratitude, and boldness. Reflect on how far you've come and celebrate the work God has done in you—spirit, mind, and body.

Weekly Prayer:
Thank You, Lord, for bringing me this far. Help me to finish strong—not in my own strength, but in Yours. Let my life reflect Your glory, and may this journey bring lasting transformation. Amen.

Day 36: God's Recipe Includes Lots of Love – Strengthening Family Bonds

Scripture Focus: "Trust in the Lord with all your heart and lean not on your own understanding; in all your ways submit to Him, and He will make your paths straight." (Proverbs 3:5-6)

Faith in Motion: The Importance of Working Together

Blending a family is not for the faint of heart. It requires patience, faith, and, above all, love. When my husband Robin and I came together as a blended family, we knew that God had brought us together for His purposes. But the journey was not without its challenges.

It's a lot like following a complicated recipe—one with unexpected ingredients you didn't know you'd have to work with. Blending a family involves more than just the couple; it means bringing together children, personalities, emotions, finances, and unforeseen circumstances. Some days, the "recipe" came together beautifully. Other days, it felt like we needed to start over from scratch.

Yet through it all, we placed God at the center. We prayed together, surrendered daily, and trusted Him to be the Master Chef of our home. Over time, He blended us in ways we could never have orchestrated on our own. "But the Holy Spirit produces this kind of fruit in our lives: love, joy, peace, patience, kindness, goodness, faithfulness, gentleness, and self-control." (Galatians 5:22-23)

Shaping Bodies & Hearts: Finding a Partner

Just as a blended family requires unity, teamwork, and patience, partner exercises in fitness require coordination, trust, and encouragement. When we work together in faith or in fitness, we strengthen one another. In fitness, working out with a partner challenges us, keeps us accountable, and allows us to push beyond what we could do alone. Similarly, in family relationships, we grow stronger when we support one another, listen, and offer encouragement.

Whether in marriage, parenting, or fitness, teamwork makes all the difference. As Ecclesiastes 4:9 reminds us, "Two are better than one, because they have a good return for their labor."

Shaping Bodies: Partner Workout for Strength and Unity

Exercising with a spouse, family member, or friend not only boosts motivation but also builds trust, strengthens relationships, and adds joy to your fitness routine. These partner exercises are designed to encourage teamwork and unity—both physically and spiritually.

Exercise: Partner Workout Routine:

- **Medicine Ball Pass (20 reps):** Stand a few feet apart and pass a weighted ball back and forth. Focus on coordination and encouragement.
- **Plank High-Fives (10 reps per side):** Get into a plank position facing each other. While holding the plank, lift one hand to high-five your partner—challenging your balance and teamwork.
- **Squat & Roll Medicine Ball (15 reps):** Perform a squat while rolling the medicine ball to your partner. They'll catch it and repeat the movement, promoting timing and trust.

Repeat the circuit 2-3 times, focusing on encouragement, laughter, and mutual support.

Shaping Hearts: Strengthening Family Bonds

Pray Together – As a family or with your spouse, ask God to deepen your love and patience.

Journal – Write down three ways you can show love to a family member this week.

Open Communication – Discuss a challenge in your family and commit to working through it with grace and prayer.

Meditate on Scripture – Reflect on **Galatians 5:22-23**–how can you cultivate these fruits in your relationships?

Dig Deeper

Be intentional about strengthening family bonds this week. Plan one activity—like a shared workout, meal, or prayer time—to connect with your spouse or a family member. Ask God to grow the fruit of His Spirit in your home and guide your hearts in love and unity.

Reflection and Prayer

Heavenly Father, thank You for the gift of family. Whether blended or not, You call us to love, support, and encourage one another. Help us to place You first in our relationships, to exercise patience, and to strengthen our bonds through faith and love. Guide us in unity and peace. In Jesus' name, amen.

My Reflections & Prayer Notes:

Day 37: Faith-Prayer-Discipline-Repeat

Scripture Focus: "For God so loved the world that he gave his one and only Son, that whoever believes in him shall not perish but have eternal life." (John 3:16)

Faith in Motion: Daily Strengthening Through Faith

Oh, the times when God's presence feels so close that we never want the experience to end! In these mountain-top moments, my strength is renewed, and I feel deeply connected to God. My inner warrior stands tall, speaks boldly, and my confidence soars like on the wings of eagles. It is in these times that I can physically feel the strength of the Lord rising within me. I am reading the Word daily, praying continually, and soaking in His presence. My cravings are for things of the Lord, and my own desires fade away. These are the best of times.

But then, there are other times when distractions, stress, and worldly influences interfere with my connection to God. I know the truth, yet in moments of weakness, I allow my thoughts, emotions, or frustrations to take over. I make decisions based on my flesh instead of faith. Guilt and condemnation soon follow, leaving me feeling drained and discouraged. These are the moments when my spiritual discipline wavers, and I need to realign myself with God's truth.

Paul addresses this struggle in Romans 7:21-25: "I have discovered this principle of life—that when I want to do what is right, I inevitably do what is wrong... Oh, what a miserable person I am! Who will free me from this life that is dominated by sin and death? Thank God! The answer is in Jesus Christ our Lord."

Before I fully committed my life to Christ, I was spiritually starving. I had no prayer life, no Bible study, and no connection to God's people. My soul was running on empty. But when I surrendered my heart to Jesus, I experienced a hunger for His Word like never before. Through faith, prayer, and discipline, my life was transformed. Just as our bodies require nourishment and training, our spirits need daily strengthening through faith.

Shaping Bodies & Hearts: Commit to the Process

Just as our spiritual lives require consistency and discipline, so does our physical fitness. If we neglect our training, our strength fades, our endurance weakens, and we struggle to perform even the simplest tasks. The same is true for our faith—when we neglect prayer, scripture, and time with God, our spiritual strength diminishes.

The key to both spiritual and physical transformation is consistency. The Apostle Paul reminds us in 1 Corinthians

9:24-27: "Don't you realize that in a race everyone runs, but only one person gets the prize? So run to win! All athletes are disciplined in their training. They do it to win a prize that will fade away, but we do it for an eternal prize."

Faith, prayer, and discipline must be practiced daily, just like a structured workout routine. The more we commit to the process, the stronger we become—both physically and spiritually.

Shaping Bodies: Repetition for Strength and Endurance

Just as repeated physical exercises build strength and stamina, our spiritual growth comes through daily repetition—prayer, scripture reading, and consistent obedience to God's Word. Discipline shapes both body and spirit.

Exercise: Discipline-Based Workout Routine:

- **Weighted Chest Press (15 reps):** Strengthens upper body muscles and reinforces commitment to steady growth.
- **Weighted Side Squats (15 reps):** Builds lower body strength and improves balance.
- **Plank Hold (30–60 seconds):** Engages the core and cultivates physical and spiritual stability.
- **Hammer Curls with Knee Drive (15 reps):** Combines strength and coordination, symbolizing persistence in your walk with Christ.

Repeat the circuit 2-3 times, focusing on control, breath, and perseverance in each repetition.

Shaping Hearts: Committing to Daily Faith Training

Be Consistent – Set aside a consistent time each day to read the Bible and pray.

Meditate on Scripture – Choose a passage of scripture to meditate on throughout the day.

Journal – Write down one area where you need more spiritual discipline and ask God for guidance.

Practice Your Faith Daily – Create a simple daily faith routine (morning prayer, evening reflection, scripture memorization) and commit to repeating it daily.

Dig Deeper

This week, reflect on how consistency in faith, prayer, and discipline strengthens your spirit, mind, and body. What routines help you stay connected to God? Identify one area where you've drifted and realign it with daily spiritual and physical discipline. Keep showing up. Repeat.

Reflection and Prayer

Heavenly Father, I desire to grow in faith, prayer, and discipline. Help me to stay consistent in my walk with You, even when distractions arise. Strengthen my spiritual endurance so that I may run the race with perseverance. Let my life reflect Your strength and truth. In Jesus' name, amen.

My Reflections & Prayer Notes:

_____

_____

_____

_____

_____

_____

_____

_____

_____

_____

_____

_____

_____

_____

Day 38: Rooted in Spiritual Habits

Scripture Focus: "Let your roots grow down into Him, and let your lives be built on Him. Then your faith will grow strong in the truth you were taught." (Colossians 2:7)

Faith in Motion: Staying Rooted in Him

Earlier this week, while my husband mowed on our farm, I stayed behind watching our two-year-old granddaughter, Eden, so her parents could rest and care for their newborn. When my husband returned, he excitedly told me about some striking plants growing on the far side of the property. Curious, he invited Eden and me to ride over and see them.

As we approached, I noticed tall, bold stalks of creamy white bell-shaped flowers. I assumed they were weeds—but they were far too lovely to dismiss. After a little research, I discovered they were *yucca plants*—hardy, drought-tolerant, evergreen, and thriving in full sun with deep roots. Though they only bloom briefly, they remain vibrant and strong through every season.

This was more than a plant discovery, it was a spiritual lesson. Like the yucca, our lives are not defined by constant blooming, productivity, or performance. God calls us to stay rooted in Him through every season, even when fruit is not immediately visible. What matters most is our foundation—our root system—in Christ.

Shaping Bodies & Hearts: What We Feed Grows

Just as the yucca thrives through deep roots and resilience, our spirits flourish when we stay anchored in God's Word and train ourselves in godliness. A strong root system—spiritually and physically—doesn't happen overnight. It takes time, pruning, intention, and consistent discipline.

In fitness, we build strength through regular movement and mindful care of our bodies. In faith, we grow through daily habits like prayer, worship, scripture reading, and guarding what we allow into our minds and hearts. What we feed grows. What we neglect weakens.

Philippians 4:8 urges us to fix our thoughts on what is true and pure. Matthew 6:22 reminds us that our eyes are lamps to our bodies. And 1 Timothy 4:8 tells us that while physical training is good, training for godliness has eternal value.

Shaping Bodies: Rooted Strength

This exercise reinforces a grounded, stable foundation—mirroring the deep spiritual roots we cultivate in Christ.

Exercise: Rooted Strength Deadlifts

- Stand tall with feet hip-width apart, holding weights in front of your thighs.
- With a flat back, hinge at the hips, and slowly lower the weights toward the floor.
- Keep your knees slightly bent and core engaged.
- Push through your heels to return to standing.

Repeat 12-15 times for 2-3 sets, visualizing your feet rooted into the ground, drawing up strength with each rep.

Shaping Hearts:

Take Inventory of Your Spiritual Garden – What thoughts or habits need pruning?

Identify 3 Spiritual Disciplines – Discover those things you want to deepen (e.g., reading the Bible daily, limiting screen time, speaking truth aloud).

Write a Declaration – For each habit you wish to improve upon, write a declaration of faith, such as: "I will guard my thoughts and fix them on Christ."

Pray – Ask the Holy Spirit to replant you in places of greater purpose and visibility for His glory.

Dig Deeper

This week, choose one spiritual habit to deepen—whether it's reading Scripture, praying, worshiping, or guarding your thoughts. Practice it daily and watch your roots grow stronger. Pair it with physical discipline by increasing your reps each day in a strength movement like squats or deadlifts. Each evening, ask yourself: "DID I GROW DEEPER ROOTS TODAY?" Let consistency anchor you in truth.

Reflection & Prayer

Father, thank You for planting me in Your truth. Help me stay rooted in You through spiritual discipline and daily faithfulness. Strengthen me through every season, not just when I feel productive or noticed. Let my roots grow deep so that my life may bear fruit in due time and glorify You. In Jesus' name, amen.

My Reflections & Prayer Notes:

_____
_____
_____
_____
_____
_____
_____
_____
_____
_____
_____

Day 39: Persevering in Purpose

Scripture Focus: "And let us run with perseverance the race marked out for us, fixing our eyes on Jesus." (Hebrews 12:1-2)

Faith in Motion: The Importance of Perseverance

There were seasons in my life when I wanted to give up. Whether it was during recovery from heart surgery, parenting through pain, or pushing through a tough workout, quitting felt easier than pressing on. But God reminded me: "You're not doing this alone. I've called you, and I will carry you." I learned that perseverance isn't about willpower; it's about trusting the One who holds your purpose.

Perseverance grows in the daily choices to keep moving forward, even when it feels hard. Just as muscles are strengthened through repeated resistance, our faith is strengthened when we lean on God again and again in trials. Fixing our eyes on Jesus keeps us from being overwhelmed by obstacles and reminds us that He already ran this race before us. Each step we take in faith is proof of His strength at work within us.

Perseverance is not about sprinting through life but running with steady faith, one step at a time. Each trial we endure and each hurdle we overcome shapes us to look more like Christ. When we fix our eyes on Jesus, He gives us the strength to keep going, not just to finish the race, but to finish it well: strong in faith, rooted in purpose, and confident in His promise.

Shaping Bodies & Hearts: Continual Trust in God

Perseverance is a muscle. Just like endurance training builds physical strength over time, spiritual perseverance is developed through continual trust in God. You may not see a breakthrough immediately, but pressing forward with purpose produces fruit that lasts.

Shaping Bodies: Endurance Training

This workout builds cardiovascular endurance and mental perseverance, mirroring our faith walk when the path feels long or difficult.

Exercise: Endurance Walk or Jog

- **Set a Timer** for 20–30 minutes.
- **Begin with a Warm-Up**: Walk at a steady pace for 3–5 minutes.
- **Use Intervals**: Walk for 2 minutes, then jog or brisk walk for 1 minute. Repeat for the duration.

- **Focus on Your Breath and Prayer**: Meditate as you move—"Let us run with perseverance the race marked out for us **(Hebrews 12:1-2)**."

As you walk or jog, imagine you are running your race of faith with endurance, keeping your eyes fixed on Jesus.

Shaping Hearts: Stay Faithful

Perseverance starts in the heart. It's not about running faster—it's about staying faithful. When the path feels long, let God's promises anchor you. He's using every step to shape your character and deepen your trust. Don't give up—your heart is being strengthened for His purpose.

Pray – Ask the Holy Spirit: *"Where do I need to persevere right now?"*

Journal – Write down any areas where you feel discouraged or weary.

Speak Truth Aloud – Declare things like, "*I will not quit. God is strengthening me for this purpose."*

Be Honest With Yourself – Reflect on how your physical endurance mirrors your spiritual growth.

Dig Deeper

Set one goal this week that aligns with your God-given purpose—whether it's to write, serve, lead, or move forward in faith. Push past a limitation or excuse that's been holding you back. Celebrate each small step as progress and remember—perseverance isn't perfection, it's obedience. You are pressing on with purpose!

Reflection & Prayer

Jesus, when I grow weary, help me keep my eyes on You. Remind me why I started, and Who walks with me. Strengthen me to persevere in my calling—not just for myself, but for those You've called me to serve. Help me press forward in faith and finish well. In Your name, amen.

My Reflections & Prayer Notes:

_____
_____
_____
_____
_____
_____
_____
_____
_____
_____
_____
_____
_____

Day 40: Finish Strong with a Kingdom Mindset

Scripture Focus: "Therefore, since we are surrounded by such a great cloud of witnesses, let us throw off everything that hinders and the sin that so easily entangles. And let us run with perseverance the race marked out for us, fixing our eyes on Jesus, the pioneer and perfecter of faith." (Hebrews 12:1-2)

Faith in Motion: Draw Near to God

We know the enemy, Satan, has come to destroy us. He will do anything and use anyone to accomplish his evil plan. In contrast, our gracious God has plans to prosper us, not to harm us—plans to give us hope and a future. Through life's challenges, I have learned that praising God and magnifying His Holy Name breaks through the enemy's dark plans. In moments of desperation, when my life felt like it was sinking, I drew closer to the Lord. It was in those trials that I learned to boldly praise Him and trust His plan.

When the storm clouds were the darkest, God became my strongest ally. As I surrendered my worries to Him and adjusted my mindset to focus on His promises, I witnessed

His plans in Jeremiah 29:11 unfold before my eyes. We all face giants—unexpected battles that threaten to shake our faith. But God grants us supernatural strength, wisdom, and discernment in how to face them.

Finishing strong requires more than physical endurance—it requires a kingdom mindset. We are not running aimlessly; we are running toward Jesus, the author and perfecter of our faith. Each obstacle becomes an opportunity to see His power at work. Each hardship reminds us that this race is not ours alone, but one we run with a great cloud of witnesses cheering us on.

As you close this 40-day journey, be encouraged: you are equipped to live with purpose, perseverance, and praise. Keep your eyes fixed on Christ, for He is your strength and your victory. Finish strong—not in your own power, but in His, knowing that the best is yet to come.

Shaping Bodies & Hearts: Finish Strong

Just as endurance is required to finish a physical race, a Kingdom mindset is necessary to finish our spiritual journey strong. In fitness, the last stretch of a workout often feels the hardest, yet pushing through builds resilience. Likewise, in faith, perseverance through trials refines and strengthens us. We are called to run the race set before us with unwavering determination.

The story of Queen Esther is a reminder of finishing strong. She stepped out in faith, risking everything to fulfill God's plan for her life. Through prayer and fasting, she gained the courage to stand against the enemy and save her people. She was born *for such a time as this* (Esther 4:14). Just like Esther, God calls us to rise with boldness and trust Him to equip us for our purpose.

Shaping Bodies: Endurance and Strength

This workout develops lasting strength and stamina—both essential to finishing strong in your faith and fitness journey.

Exercise: Endurance-Focused Workout Routine:

- **Plank with Shoulder Taps (1-2 minutes):** Strengthens core and upper body while reinforcing balance and control. Tap each shoulder slowly, maintaining stability.
- **Alternate Reverse Lunges with Overhead Press (15 reps per leg):** Step back into a lunge while pressing weights overhead, symbolizing strength rising from a grounded foundation.
- **Kettlebell Deadlift to High Pull (15 reps):** Engage your glutes and core, pulling the kettlebell to chest height—mirroring how God lifts us up when we rely on His strength.
- **Kettlebell Swing with Reverse Lunge (15 reps):** Combine power and control, swinging the kettlebell forward and stepping back into a lunge.

Repeat 2-3 times, focusing on steady breathing and the strength God provides to persevere.

Shaping Hearts: Declaring Victory and Running the Race

- Declare God's promises over your life daily, using scriptures like **Isaiah 54:17**: *"No weapon formed against you shall prosper."*
- Spend time in prayer, asking God to give you the endurance to finish strong.
- Write down one area in your life where you need a Kingdom mindset shift.
- Choose one day this week to fast and dedicate time to seeking God's direction.

Finish Strong

As you close out this 40-day journey, take a moment to look back and give thanks. Every step, every stretch, every scripture has brought you closer to the heart of God. You've pressed through physical challenges, grown in spiritual strength, and shaped your spirit, mind, and body with intention.

Now it's time to run the final stretch with boldness.

- **Declare Victory:** Speak God's promises over your life. You are more than a conqueror through Christ (**Romans 8:37**).
- **Live with Intention:** Ask God for clarity as you step into the next season—aligning your daily choices with His purpose.

- **Finish Strong in Faith and Fitness:** Keep moving. Keep praying. Keep trusting. The same God who brought you this far will carry you forward.
- **Pass it On:** Encourage someone else to begin their journey of transformation. Share your story. Be a light.

You were made for this race. Keep your eyes on Jesus, the Author and Finisher of your faith. Victory is already written into your story—now walk it out, strong to the finish!

Reflection and Prayer

Heavenly Father, thank You for calling me to run this race with perseverance. Strengthen my faith so that I may finish strong, keeping my eyes fixed on You. Let my life be a testimony of Your power and faithfulness. I declare that no weapon formed against me will prosper. I trust in Your plan and run forward in victory. In Jesus' name, amen.

My Reflections & Prayer Notes:

_____
_____
_____
_____
_____
_____

Conclusion: Keep Moving Forward in the Strength of the Lord

Congratulations on completing *Shaped By Faith: A Devotional for Strengthening Your Spirit, Mind, & Body*! This is not the finish line—it's the **beginning** of a lifelong journey of living aligned with God's purpose. Every step you've taken, every challenge you've faced, and every victory you've experienced are shaping you into the person God created you to be.

God calls us to move **forward**, not backward. There will be days when you feel strong, and others when you struggle—but remember: *"My grace is sufficient for you, for my power is made perfect in weakness."* (2 Corinthians 12:9) Keep pressing on, knowing that **He equips you** for the race ahead.

Encouragement to Keep Going

- **Stay Rooted in the Word** – Let Scripture be your daily nourishment.

- **Prioritize Prayer** – Talk with God often and listen for His voice.

- **Commit to Whole-Person Strength** – Continue exercising both body and spirit.

- **Encourage Others** – Share what God has done in you and be a light.

- **Never Give Up** – The race is not over. Keep your eyes on Jesus, the author and perfecter of your faith.

A Final Blessing

May the Lord strengthen you as you walk in faith.
May He equip you with endurance to press forward,
wisdom to make godly choices,
and courage to face every challenge ahead.

May your **spirit, mind, and body** be *shaped by faith,*
bringing glory to God in all you do.

"But those who hope in the Lord will renew their strength.
They will soar on wings like eagles;
they will run and not grow weary,
they will walk and not be faint." – Isaiah 40:31

Go forward in His strength—and finish your race well.

With you on this journey,
In His Strength,
Theresa Rowe

Next Steps: Living Shaped By Faith

You've completed 40 days of aligning your spirit, mind, and body with God's Word—but the journey continues.

Take a moment to reflect:

What has God taught me over these 40 days?

How has my relationship with Him grown?

What spiritual or physical habits do I want to continue?

Who can I encourage or disciple with what I've learned?

Write your answers below and recommit to continuing the journey—faithfully and intentionally.

_____

_____

_____

_____

_____

_____

_____

_____

My Reflections & Prayer Notes

(Use this space to write your thoughts, prayers, or takeaways as you continue walking in faith. Reflect on how God has shaped your spirit, mind, and body through this devotional.)

_____

_____

_____

_____

_____

_____

_____

_____

_____

_____

_____

_____

_____

_____

_____

_____

Stay Connected with Shaped By Faith

Scan the QR code and visit ShapedByFaith.com to explore devotionals, blog posts, books, faith-based products, and the latest details about where to watch or listen to *Shaped By Faith*. You'll also find information about Theresa's speaking ministry and how to invite her to share at your conference, retreat, or women's event.

📺 Television:

Shaped By Faith is broadcast on more than 18 television networks nationwide, with new stations being added regularly. A few of these networks are NRB TV, CTN – Christian Television Network, WLMB-TV 40 (Toledo, OH), WATC The Point (Atlanta, GA), and Canyon Star TV. For the most up-to-date listings, visit the website at ShapedByFaith.com. Episodes are also shared weekly on the Shaped By Faith YouTube Channel.

🎧 Radio & Podcasts:

The Shaped By Faith radio show continues to expand and is now carried on multiple radio stations across the country, with more being added regularly. You can also listen anytime on demand through Rumble, Spotify, iHeart Radio, Amazon Music, Apple Podcasts, Canyon Star TV, and

ChristianMix106. For the latest radio listings, visit ShapedByFaith.com.

📩 **Newsletter & Social:**

Stay encouraged throughout the week by signing up for the *Shaped By Faith* newsletter ShapedByFaith.com. For daily Scripture, faith-filled encouragement, and behind-the-scenes inspiration, follow @shapedbyfaith on social media.

Blessings,
Theresa

From My Heart to Yours

Thank you for walking through this 40-day journey with me. I have prayed over every word and every exercise, trusting that God would meet you right where you are. I pray this devotional has helped you grow stronger—not only in your body but in your faith and your identity in Christ.

Let your next steps be guided by this truth:

God is still shaping your body and heart for His purposes—one day, one decision, one prayer at a time.

With all my heart,

Theresa

218

About the Author

Theresa Rowe is the founder of Shaped By Faith, a Christian fitness ministry that blends faith and fitness to equip women for God's purposes. She is a nationally recognized TV and radio host, author, and speaker whose testimony of healing, perseverance, and joy in the Lord inspires audiences worldwide. Through every workout, devotional, and message, Theresa's mission is clear: to help others grow stronger – spirit, mind, and body – for the glory of God.

www.ingramcontent.com/pod-product-compliance
Lightning Source LLC
Chambersburg PA
CBHW060512100426
42743CB00009B/1291